The Internship Advantage

Get Real-World Job Experience to Launch Your Career

Dario Bravo and Carol Whiteley

PRENTICE HALL PRESS

The Berkley Publishing Group
Published by the Penguin Group
Penguin Group (USA) Inc.
375 Hudson Street, New York, New York 10014 USA
Penguin Group (Canada), 90 Eglinton Avenue, Suite 700, Toronto, Ontario M4P 2YR, Canada
(a division of Pearson Penguin Canada, Inc.)
Penguin Books Ltd., 80 Strand, London WC2R 0RL, England
Penguin Group Ireland, 25 St. Stephen's Green, Dublin 2, Ireland
(a division of Penguin Books Ltd.)
Penguin Group (Australia), 250 Camberwell Road, Camberwell, Victoria 3124, Australia
(a division of Pearson Australia Group Pty. Ltd.)
Penguin Books India Pvt. Ltd., 11 Community Centre, Panchsheel Park, New Delhi—
110 017, India
Penguin Group (NZ), cnr. Airborne and Rosedale Roads, Albany, Auckland 1310, New Zealand
(a division of Pearson New Zealand Ltd.)
Penguin Books (South Africa) (Pty.) Ltd., 24 Sturdee Avenue, Rosebank, Johannesburg 2196,
South Africa
Penguin Books Ltd., Registered Offices: 80 Strand, London WC2R 0RL, England

PRINTING HISTORY
Prentice Hall press trade paperback edition / September 2005

Prentice Hall Press is a registered trademark of Penguin Group (USA) Inc.

The Library of Congress Cataloging-in-Publication Data

Bravo, Dario.
    The internship advantage / Dario Bravo and Carol Whiteley.
       p. cm.
    ISBN 0-7352-0391-1
    1. Internship programs.   I. Whiteley, Carol.   II. Title.
    LC1072.I58B73 2005
    311.25'922—dc22   2005043041

PRINTED IN THE UNITED STATES OF AMERICA

10   9   8   7   6   5   4   3   2   1

Acknowledgments

To Carol Roth and Carol Whiteley for their unwavering encouragement and support in making this book a reality. To Alex White, who gave me the opportunity to begin my career at UCLA in 1985, for which I offer him my heartfelt thanks. To Kathy Sims, the director of the UCLA Career Center—I am especially grateful for her support. I would also like to acknowledge my colleagues at the Career Center who through humor and sincerity have been supportive in this endeavor. I would also like to thank Karol Johansen for her contribution and assistance and for the materials and contacts she provided, and Don Spring, our librarian, for the reference materials he provided. A special thanks to Eric Baldwin, our local counselor, for preparing the Will Intern résumés for the book; Chet Wang for his assistance preparing the CD; Eva Walthers, our most esteemed international counselor, for all of her expertise and her contribution to the information on international programs; and my friends at Myrtun Corporation, especially Abel Stephen. Finally, my gratitude to all of the UCLA students and to the UCLA alumni of our different programs, employers, and organizations who provide opportunities to our students for contributing to and supporting *The Internship Advantage*.

Dario Bravo

A book with the scope of this one would never have been written without the help, expertise, and enthusiasm of many people. But before I thank them all, I want to single out a special few. Dario Bravo was a pleasure to work with, not only as an expert on internships but a counselor devoted to helping students blossom, succeed, and grow. Carol Susan Roth, my agent, did a wonderful job putting this project together and guiding it to reality. My son, Mark, my daughter-in-law, Trina, and my dad, Bernie, were terrific supporters. And Jimmy, my GLL, was a constant source of advice, encouragement, and love.

I also gratefully acknowledge the following wonderful people who provided me with their insights, stories, energy, and information: Georgia Kleeman-Keller, Gabrielle Fardwell, Rosa Jimenez, Theresa Luong, Ana Martini, Robert Tse, Nancy Romero, Jane Chongchit, Don Terpstra, Jeff Kline, Cherie Green, Leif-Eric Easley, Ian Taggart, Alice Kleeman, Eric Baldwin, Murray Suid, and Frank McKinney.

Carol Whiteley

Contents

How to Get Real-World Job Experience and Find a Career That You'll Love

I f you've been having a hard time deciding what you want to do with your life—or if you've decided but just can't seem to wedge your foot in the working-world door—you're in good company. Many of the more than 15,000,000 students who will be pouring out of colleges, graduate schools, and professional schools this year have no idea what their next step should be, and more than 8,700,000 other people are currently unemployed. There's a large percentage of people out there who are wandering the streets wondering, "What in the world do I want to do and how in the world can I land a spot to do it in?"

Some of these people, maybe you included, are talking to career counselors, posting résumés online, and going to job fairs yet are still feeling uncertain. But many of these people don't know that there's a proven, exciting way both to identify their passion *and* to get a good job in their field of interest: by doing one or more internships.

Just what is an internship? It's work experience that complements your academic training or introduces you to a new career or field of interest as well as to professionals in that field. It's a job that lets you apply your classroom learning in a real-world setting and gives you responsibilities and ways to grow that are similar to an entry-level position. But an internship is not a job in which you just answer phones or spend the day filing. It's an opportunity to gain knowledge and develop real skills related to a goal or interest and to prepare you for and help you land a full-time job in the working world.

Internships, in fact, are now the number one way that employers take on new hires, ahead of job fairs, employee referrals, on-campus recruiting, Internet job postings, and co-op programs; Microsoft alone offers full-time employment to more than four hundred interns from its program each year. Internships are also an incredible opportunity to learn about yourself, stretch your boundaries, make connections, open doors, get that all-important experience that every potential employer says you've got to have, make you more marketable, and see if the path you're on is leading to happiness and fulfillment. If it's not, other internships will help you check out other possible fields; they let you try careers on for size before you commit to buying.

Doesn't it simply make sense? Two former interns think it does:

My internship at the Smithsonian was amazing—it sparked my passion for museums and history. Not only did I work right there in that prestigious museum, but I was given the opportunity to work on a book a senior curator was writing. I loved the experience so much, and made so many friends and contacts, that after the internship was over I made the decision to stay on in Washington. Now I'm getting full-time-job interviews at museums all over the city because of my Smithsonian internship. The experience was not only wonderful, but it helped me to begin to figure out where I wanted my career path to take me—and it put me on that path.

My internship allowed me to grow and mature, gain experience, make new friends, and learn something new. But it also made me aware of career possibilities that I hadn't considered before. If I hadn't done an internship, I would never have decided to join the Lobby Corps, and learn to lobby for student issues at the local, state, and national level. And that experience led me to finding my passion—serving people through the political system.

Both of those students found a career and a calling by taking part in internships they landed through the UCLA (University of California at Los Angeles) Internship and Study Abroad Services program. The unique, acclaimed program has been in existence for more than forty years and has placed more than ten thousand students and alumni in challenging and satisfying local, state, national, and international internships in which they have not only grown but from which they have launched themselves into productive and passionate lives.

Their success can be yours. Even if you're not currently a student. And even if you've been part of the work force for some time. Internships—and related opportunities for graduates—are available in just about every career area and every part of the country (there are options abroad too), and they aren't restricted to students in their teens and twenties. You can be a grandparent and see what it's like to teach in a foreign country. You can have worked in the same job for several years and do a fellowship in a different field that sounds more exciting. The wonderful thing about internships and related options is that just about anyone can take advantage of the world of possibilities they offer.

But how do you get started? Why, with the book you're holding in your hands! Based on the hugely successful UCLA program, this book tells you everything you need to know about internships and related opportunities:

- The different types that are available

- How to figure out your particular skills and talents

- How to find quality internship programs, even if you're not a student, and to open yourself to new places and new possibilities

- How to narrow down the choices

- What employers are looking for

- How to land the internship you really want

- How to finance the internship if it's not paid

- How to make the most of the ten or twelve weeks the typical internship runs

- How to figure out if you're on the right track—or if it's time to try another direction

- How to turn the experience into a full-time job that will make you cheer

There are also plenty of stories and advice from current and former interns—what to do and what *not* to do—to help you use your internship to the best possible advantage. And if you're a college administrator or a potential employer of interns, you'll find all the information you need, based on the UCLA model, to develop a comprehensive and successful internship program of your own.

Deciding what you want to do with your life can be very difficult; you probably know that already. And finding a job that not only lets you earn a living but makes you happy to go to work in the morning may seem like something that's next to impossible. But there is a way to try careers on for size while you learn, gain real-world experience, experiment, network and find mentors, change, move ahead, and grow. So don't wait any longer—too many graduating seniors come to the end of their college careers and realize only then, and much to their regret, that an internship could have pointed them toward a new and exciting part of their lives. And too many unhappy employees continue to hold down unfulfilling jobs because they don't think it's possible to venture down a more satisfying path.

Don't let that happen to you. Read on to discover how an internship can be a fun, fast, successful way to find a great job and a life that you'll love.

Chapter 1
What Internships Can Do for You

As a UCLA undergraduate, Lisa made the most of her college years. She took exciting and challenging classes in her major, political science. She wrote for the school newspaper. She joined a number of clubs and took part in a wide variety of activities. She developed wonderful, lasting friendships. She learned to speak Chinese.

But when it came time to graduate, she had no idea what she wanted to do, of the direction she wanted her life to take. Like many of her political science classmates, she had a vague notion of entering some area of public policy work or looking for a spot in government service. But though her classes had been outstanding, they had been heavy on theory and pretty much lacking in hands-on experience and skills building; she didn't know if this was really a field she wanted to pursue or had the talent for. At one point Lisa had even considered changing her major to economics or computer science because they seemed more likely to help prepare her for the working world. But she had enjoyed and stayed with political science, and now, there she was, a graduating senior, facing what so many graduating students—and others—face: figuring out what the right career path is and how to build a passionate life that will fulfill them.

Sound familiar? It's a situation most of us struggle with at some point in our lives, and one that we can feel incredibly ill-equipped to handle. How do I get where I want to go? How do I even figure out what it is I want to do?

Happily for Lisa, help was right there on campus. Just before she was about to graduate, she made her way to UCLA's Internship and Study Abroad Services campus office, through which she applied for and won an internship position at the University of California's Office of Federal Relations, in Washington, D.C. She hoped the experience, interning in California's lobbying office on Capitol Hill, would give her the skills and the know-how she needed to find a job in the government sector—a start down what she thought might be the right career path. And the job did give her the opportunity to develop skills, gain confidence, and learn what being part of a public-service program was really like. But her internship did more for her than that. It allowed her to experience the commitment and enthusiasm of dedicated professionals. It let her observe how even people with opposing perspectives and diverse backgrounds solved problems and worked together with respect. And it opened her eyes to new ways in which individuals can contribute to the general good as well as inspired her to explore possibilities outside traditional public service roles.

In other words, it gave her experience, opened doors, and encouraged her to grow and experiment. And it led to a full-time job, which set her on a course to her true calling: teaching special-education classes for children of immigrant families. In Lisa's own words, "My internship broadened my perspective, started the process of exploration that eventually put me on the right career path, and has paid longer-lasting dividends than almost any other experience I've had."

Sound almost too good to be true? It's not. For millions of people, high school and college students and graduates alike, internships have proven to be eye-opening, door-opening experiences that lead to discovery, opportunities, networks, and knowledge—not to mention challenging careers, a head start into grad school, and the chance to find and pursue their passions.

Of course, not every internship is perfect (and in case you land in one of the imperfect ones we give you lots of pointers for dealing with it in Chapter 9). And a great one isn't just going to fall into your lap—you're going to have to do some research, take the initiative, fill out applications, go through interviews, and persevere. But we're going to help you every step of the way to find and win an exciting internship and then use it as a springboard to a great job and a fulfilling life. We're going to help you get the internship advantage.

How does that advantage work? In addition to all the opportunities we've mentioned for personal growth, it maximizes your chances and makes you a front-runner when it comes to landing a full-time job. That's because:

- Interns have on-the-job experience that employers wish each applicant had but doesn't. Especially in highly competitive fields, hands-on experience will set you apart from applicants with only classroom training. For example, if you volunteer with the Peace Corps to help entrepreneurs in eastern European countries get their businesses off the ground, you'll be able to start a job with knowledge that otherwise might take months of on-the-job training—and expense to the employer—to learn. Internships solve the age-old dilemma of needing experience to get the job but not being able to get a job to get the experience.

- Interns stand out among other high achievers: Many students graduate with a 4.0 grade-point average (GPA), but job applicants with a high GPA and an internship on their résumés will jump to the top of the call list.

- Interns develop networks and contacts that make it not only easier for them to learn about job opportunities but be recommended for positions to boot. Jim, for example, did an internship with a TV station because he thought he wanted a career in broadcast journalism but after the experience realized that the field wasn't for him. A friend he made during the summer program later told Jim about an opening in his business-consulting firm and recommended him for the position. After graduating, Jim applied for and got the job. Even though his internship had been in a different field, his new employers liked the fact that he had real-world experience under his belt and that one of their employees knew he was a solid guy—and Jim has been enjoying his new direction ever since.

• People who have completed internships have already discovered whether or not they like the field. Doing an internship lets you see firsthand if the career path you *think* you want is really the career path you truly want. That not only makes you a more enthusiastic candidate but saves you the time and pain of giving your all to get a job just to find out it's not a match—and that you need to quit and start again. If you've already done an internship in the field, your employer will also be more likely to think you're someone who'll stay in the position for some time to come—a definite point in your favor.

• Employers hire their interns. Especially in a tight economy, employers are more likely to hire successful interns who have proven themselves in the work environment than to take a chance on a job seeker who has no experience and whom they've just met. According to the National Association of Colleges and Employers, more than 38 percent of all interns are offered full-time positions after they complete their internship.

• Job applicants who can show up on the first day of work with direct experience and career-oriented skills can often negotiate a higher starting salary than those with only classroom training.

• An internship can greatly increase your confidence in your abilities. When you apply for a job you'll already have learned some skills, and you'll be more ready and able to take on the challenges of the working world.

Ready to become an intern? These famous former interns, and the places they did their internships, may inspire you:

- Oprah Winfrey: at WTVF-TV in Nashville

- Katie Couric: at a Washington, D.C., radio station

- Dick Clark: at station WRUN in New York City

- Brooke Shields: at the San Diego Zoo

- Kiefer Sutherland: at the Williamstown Theater Festival in Williamstown, Massachusetts

- Spike Lee: at Columbia Pictures

- Steven Bochco (TV writer): at Universal Studios

- Patrick Ewing: with the Senate Finance Committee

- Bill Clinton: in the office of Senator J. William Fulbright of Arkansas

- Madeline Albright: at the *Denver Post*

- Al Gore: at the *New York Times*

- Bill Bradley: on Capitol Hill

- Ronald Reagan: at station WOC in Davenport, Iowa

- Leonard Downie (editor-in-chief of the *Washington Post*): at the *Washington Post*

- Mike Wallace: at the *Brookline Citizen* in Brookline, Massachusetts

- Carl Bernstein: at the *Washington Star*

- Bill Gates: as a Congressional page

- Donald Trump: as a construction worker for his father's Trump Corporation

If you're already part of that working world, there's something else an internship can do for you: It can lead to your becoming happier and feeling more fulfilled. A lot of people out there, maybe you too, don't enjoy the work they do and feel a good deal less than excited about the life they're leading. But their job pays the bills, and they may think they don't have the skills or the opportunity to find more fulfilling, more enjoyable work.

But living paycheck to paycheck or working day after day in a joyless environment can make you pretty miserable. If you're not happy with the work you do, and you'd like to make a change, an internship can be the way to test the waters and see what else is out there. We encourage you to do it—to take a chance on finding something better, something that makes you happy to wake up in the morning. (See Chapter 6 for lots of options for graduates and career changers.) It might be a little scary, especially if you have a family to take care of, but deciding to take a chance and move on and find an internship in an interesting-sounding field just might lead to a job that not only pays the bills but taps into your passion as well.

So don't wait any longer and don't put off looking for an internship until the last minute; many internships have early application deadlines and the application process can take a while. In addition, if you do an internship early enough in a field that turns out not to be for you, you'll still have plenty of time to try another internship in another area. Start using the information in this book now to give yourself the internship advantage and to get the inside track to finding a career you'll love. You may be like Oprah Winfrey, who interned at a TV station in Nashville and is now the queen of daytime TV; or like Bill Gates, who interned as a Congressional page but decided on a new direction and started a little company called Microsoft; or like Donald Trump, who was born into a building empire but decided he wanted to be part of it by learning the business (literally) from the ground up. Whichever career you decide on, an internship can help you find your way.

Chapter 2
Discover Your Dreams and Your Talents

OK, you've decided to take the plunge: You're going to give yourself the internship advantage. But where do you start? What's the right direction?

A good way to begin is to think about who you are, what your dreams are, and what your talents are. For some people, this is a snap. For example, take Robert. Since he was little, he has loved to draw and paint. When he was in junior high, he painted murals on the school walls, and in high school he drew cartoons for the school newspaper. Now that he's in college, his design classes are his favorite. He dreams of a life illustrating books or working for a graphic-design firm, and because he enjoys being with friends and always meets project deadlines, he thinks he'd be suited to a career in publishing or design. Robert plans to look for internships in those areas and may look into other art-related internships to broaden his perspective. He's pretty certain of who he is, where his skills lie, and which career field would make him happiest.

But then there's Rosa. Growing up, she had a million interests. She sang with the school chorus, was heavily into sports, loved baby-sitting for her younger brother and sister, read insatiably, liked to organize outings with friends, enjoyed cooking with her family—and graduated from college with a liberal arts degree. For several years after college, she worked in sales in a store near her home. But for the last year or so, she's realized that she's not very happy with her life and she doesn't feel fulfilled.

Rosa would like to make a change, but she's not at all sure which direction to take. Several friends have encouraged her to look into their lines of work, but Rosa doesn't know if she has the skills for those jobs or if a career in one of those fields would make her any happier.

If you're more like Robert, you already have a sense of which career areas you'd like to check out for internships. While you shouldn't rule out anything that sounds appealing, even if it's not in a field you've always thought was for you—internships are about stretching your boundaries and taking advantage of opportunities to grow as well as getting real experience in a career area you already know you enjoy—you have a good idea of which direction to start out in.

If you're more like Rosa, though, you're going to need to do a little more reflecting, a little more exploration, a little more consideration. But there are several ways to do this, and several resources to help you discover your strengths and your passions.

Assessment Tests

One of the best ways to pinpoint just where your talents lie and the kind of situation your personality best suits you for is to take one or more assessment tests. For example, at UCLA, the two tests most often administered are the Myers-Briggs Type Indicator® (MBTI) and the Strong Interest Inventory® (SII).

Myers-Briggs Type Indicator

According to its publisher, Consulting Psychologists Press, the MBTI is the most widely used personality inventory in the world, taken by nearly two million people every year. The test measures the taker's psychological preferences based on four basic character traits: extrovert/introvert, sensate/intuitive, thinking/feeling, and judging/perceiving. The various combinations of these preferences result in sixteen different personality types, each of which has characteristics frequently associated with it. By taking the test, you discover your personality type and the characteristics often related to it. And knowing those traits can help you think about which careers might suit you best.

For example, after answering the questions on the test, it might turn out that you're an INTJ—an introvert (I) who is intuitive (N), is thoughts (T) rather than feelings based, and more judging (J) or judicious than perceptive or open to exploring. If you look up the profile for an INTJ, you will see descriptions like "insightful, conceptual, and creative" and "independent, trusting their own judgments and perceptions more than others'." After reading more about the type (check out David Keirsey's *Please Understand Me II* or Sandra Hirsh and Jean Kummerow's *LifeTypes*) or discussing it with a counselor, you would be able to see which career paths might be good matches. For instance, if you're insightful, conceptual, creative, and independent, you might be happiest in a job in which you have a good deal of autonomy and work for positive change, perhaps a psychologist, researcher, or university professor. If you're an ESFJ (extrovert, sensate, feeling, and judging) and enjoy being with and helping other people, you might want to look for an internship in education or with a social services agency.

If you're a student, it's very likely that your college or university internship office or career center will have a copy of the MBTI test for you to take; a counselor there will help you interpret your profile. If you're not in school, you can check your local library, take a class at a nearby community college or adult education center that includes taking the test and discussing the results with a trained professional, or check the Yellow Pages for a career counselor or coach who might be able to test you and talk about possible directions. Or you can order the test and interpretive materials directly from the publisher (you might be able to share the cost with other friends who'd like to know more about themselves too):

Consulting Psychologists Press, Inc.
3803 East Bayshore Road
P.O. Box 10096
Palo Alto, CA 94303
Telephone: 650-969-8901; 800-624-1765

You can also order materials online at www.cpp-db.com.

If you want to learn more about the test before ordering materials or answering the questions, you can read up on it online at www.personalitypathways.com/type_inventory.html. You can also learn more about your type by answering the sixty-question inventory at www.personalitypage.com/indicate.html. To take the MBTI online, go to www.teamtechnology.co.uk/mbti.html. There you can order the online questionnaire and receive instructions on completing it. The purchase price includes an hour of phone consultation with a qualified expert who will discuss the results of your completed questionnaire.

If you're not sure which direction to try, the MBTI can be invaluable in helping you find a career road that suits the car you're driving. Plus it's fun, educational, and horizon widening—just like quality internships.

Strong Interest Inventory

The goal of the SII is to match your interests with a career. Rather than focus on your personality traits, though it does consider personal styles, this test measures your interest in a large number of occupations, work activities, leisure activities, and school subjects. It then compares your interest levels with the interests of thousands of people who enjoy and are successful in their jobs. The idea is that if people with interests similar to yours are happy and fulfilled doing the work they do, then it's likely you will be too.

Taking the SII is a great way to start your search for an enriching internship or to help you narrow down the field of choices. It identifies highly suitable career areas as well as other compatible fields and provides helpful job descriptions so you can start thinking about those careers right away. The three-hundred-question survey is great for students as well as those already in the work force who are looking to make a change and those returning to work after taking a break.

Like the MBTI, the SII is usually available through college and university internship and career centers, and counselors there should be able to help you evaluate your results. If you're not in school, a career coach or counselor may be able to test you, or you can order the test and other helpful materials directly from the publisher, Consulting Psychologists Press (see contact information on page 14). If you'd like to consider your interests *and* your personality traits as you start to think about career areas, the publisher offers packages that combine the MBTI and the SII.

Other Assessment Tests

Although the MBTI and the SII are the assessment tests most often administered by career counselors, there are a number of other tests available to assess personalities and careers. One book that's widely read by job hunters is *What Color Is My Parachute?,* by Richard Nelson Bolles. In addition to lots of tips about finding a great career, the book contains an exercise that helps readers zoom in on the job of their dreams. Called the "Flower Exercise," the activity asks you to write seven short stories and gives you guidance on using them to find an exciting career direction. The exercise includes determining the salary you'd like to make, where you'd like to work, and other

TEN TOP WAYS TO ASSESS YOUR INTERESTS

- Think about yourself as someone you're getting to know. Look for the things that grab your interest and get you excited.

- Ask yourself if you enjoy doing something because it's what others like to do. Try to distinguish between what society encourages and what you really want to do.

- Take an honest look at your skills and acknowledge your limitations.

- If you feel you're already on a career path but aren't sure it's the right one, don't be afraid to make a change.

- Think of a career that sounds exciting and match up your skills with the skills that would be needed.

- Think about any life dreams you've had and see if they still seem relevant. Sometimes old dreams need to be updated because of changes that have taken place.

- Make a list of what you think are your strong points. Then do some free-associating and see where they lead you.

- Think of five experiences you've had in the last year that have piqued your curiosity or been completely enjoyable. Determine if there's something they all had in common.

- Pull out all the stops to learn more about yourself. Talk to your mentor and others and use every available resource.

- Volunteer or work in an area that seems to interest you to see if it's a true path to follow.

more on-the-job issues, but it also helps you focus on your strongest interests, values, and goals.

Other books, such as *LifeTypes* and *Please Understand Me II*, mentioned earlier, and *Do What You Are,* by Paul D. Tieger and Barbara Barron-Tieger, contain exercises and information that can help you pinpoint your skills, temperament, and dreams. Check with your university or local library for more suggestions of useful books to read.

Counselors and Coaches

If you're a student, you can head to your school's career center for help with uncovering your talents and possible interests. Counselors may give you one of the assessment tests described earlier, but they will also discuss the classes you're taking, your background and experience, outside activities you're involved in, your work style, and your strong likes and dislikes. They'll guide you toward seeing which kinds of things pique your interest. Career counselors and life coaches can do the same if you're not a student; check the Yellow Pages or go online for counselors and coaches in your area.

Career Guides

Sometimes it can be helpful to work in the reverse direction: Instead of learning about your strengths and passions and using them as a springboard to a possible career, you can learn about possible careers and consider whether you've got the interests and skills to pursue them. Many career guides are available that provide in-depth descriptions of a variety of jobs, giving you a feel for what they might be like. Career centers and libraries will have tons of these books, plus online career-oriented Web sites like www.vault.com also make them available for download. Once you read through several career descriptions, you can think about how your personal style might suit them. For example, if you discover that working as a news anchor or reporter involves not only speaking to an audience on-air but writing, researching, producing, and interviewing, you might realize that communicating in a variety of ways is something you love to do and something you're good at; your talents might be perfect for a career in TV news.

Other resources are also available that use your college major as a launch pad. There are general books, such as *Major Options: The Student's Guide to Linking Majors and Career Opportunities during and after College,* by Nicholas Basta; and books for specific majors, such as *Great Jobs for Art Majors,* by Blythe Camenson; *Great Jobs for English Majors,* by Julie DeGalan and Stephen Lambert; *Career Opportunities in Computers and Cyberspace,* by Harry Henderson; *Opportunities in Biotechnology Careers,* by Sheldon S. Brown and Mark Rowh; and *Great Jobs for Political Science Majors,* by Mark Rowh. You can read about the possibilities in several different fields and see if some spark an interest or resurrect a neglected dream.

Employers, Professors, Alums, Colleagues, Friends—and Even Your Parents

If you're not sure of your talents and passions, the people who interact with you on a daily basis just might be. For example, if you have a part-time job, your employer can probably tell you where you shine: You're able to work on your own without a lot of direction and love giving new co-workers a helping hand—great traits for being an independent management consultant. Or you enjoy strategizing solutions to problems and like to debate with co-workers—characteristics a lawyer might find important. Professors you've gotten to know in classes you particularly enjoy may also have some good insights—you do your best work writing essays and papers and seem less comfortable addressing the class or presenting information.

Alumni who graduated in your same major or who work in a field you think sounds interesting may also be helpful sources for zeroing in on your talents and interests. They can tell you about the work they're doing now, the skills they're employing, and the kind of atmosphere they work in—which may turn you off or make you think, "That sounds really exciting, I'd love to do that!" Your college or university alumni association or your high school career center can put you in touch with alums in different fields who are willing to share their thoughts and experiences with students.

If you're part of the work force, you have a built-in audience of people who would love to tell you your talents—for better or for worse! Be brave and ask them where you think your greatest strengths lie; they work with you every day, and should have a good idea of your work style and temperament. It's also possible that over coffee or while waiting for a fax to come through you discussed some of your dreams or goals with them, something that they may remember but you've forgotten under the pressures of getting by.

Your friends are another great source of information and insight. They know the real you and can help you pinpoint the things you enjoy most; you're also very likely to have shared your dreams and wishes with them. And your parents and siblings know the real you too, and though they may be a bit biased, you may want to add their thoughts to the mix. Ask them, or anyone else whose opinion you respect, for a straightforward assessment of your skills. You might be surprised by what they say, and it could lead you in a direction you've never considered before.

Your Very Own Self

After you've taken an assessment test, read through some books, looked at some Web sites, and talked to as many people as you can, it's a great idea to take some time to consider your own thoughts and feelings. While you may not be sure of exactly what your skills and strongest interests are, it's more than likely that you've been drawn to certain things or have noticed you're pretty good in certain areas. Think about those things some more and see if you can uncover a secret desire or passion—to be a teacher, to direct a television show, to make a medical breakthrough, to design the next generation of cell phones. Ask yourself, "If I could do anything, what would it be?" Nothing is too crazy; explore all the possibilities. And remember that while information from other people and other resources can be invaluable, in the end it's your life, and you need to be fulfilled living it.

Putting It All Together

One person who took advantage of the many ways to discover her talents is Ana Sanchez. Before choosing an internship, Ana talked to friends and family and to internship center staff, and thought long and hard about what her interests were. Then she did a lot of research and continued her career exploration during the several internships she completed. Here is her story:

When Ana Sanchez counsels undergraduates as a volunteer for the UCLA Alumni Association, she tells them that the best thing they can do for themselves is to do an internship. And the more internships they do, she says, the better off they'll be.

Ana is living proof that her theory is right. Today, after completing four internships during her four years in college, she's discovered her passion and holds a dream job: an associate director of a top-rated TV talk show.

Though she now says she wishes she started doing internships in high school, to get an even greater edge, Ana interned for the first time during the summer after her freshman year at college. Two of her siblings and several of her friends had done internships, and they told her they were great ways to get experience, see other parts of the country, and learn about varied ways of life. So she took their advice, and started to research opportunities.

When she began to look, Ana was pretty certain she wanted a career in the entertainment field. One job she had in mind was to be an entertainment lawyer. So she went through books and binders of entertainment and media internships at her college's internship center and then studied the Web sites of several possible companies. One of those possibilities was at the CBS television network, where a general internship was being offered—one that matched her criteria. It was a summer opening, so she could devote all her time to it, and it was at a major network where she could get exposure to a wide variety of careers, people, and opportunities. The internship wasn't paid, which was a major drawback, but Ana realized that getting a chance to see what working at a TV station was really like and finding out first-hand what directors and writers and producers and lawyers actually do completely outweighed the lack of a stipend. But she would get credit for the program, so she wouldn't be lengthening her school career. Because she had started her search early, she was able to get her application in before the deadline and won the summer internship.

She was thrilled. But she quickly learned that glamour wasn't a big part of the job. "In a lot of internships," she says, "and especially in your first one, you're going to get the coffee and answer phones and do a lot of photocopying. But the more you do, the more responsibility you're going to get."

Ana got great exposure to a whole new side of the entertainment business. When she started interning at CBS, she knew only about what went on in front of the camera. Her thoughts of being an entertainment lawyer had already lessened, but she wondered if being a reporter or an anchor, like Tom Brokaw or Katie Couric, might be the perfect job and life.

Her internship showed her that there was a lot more to TV work than she had ever imagined. TV studios had accountants and writers and editors and producers and camera operators and publicists and salespeople, as well as reporters and anchors; and interning at CBS gave her the opportunity to check out what went on in those people's day-to-day work lives. "How else would you get access to such a huge range of careers and experience, and the chance to interact with people in positions you might like to be in one day?" Ana asks students.

Over the course of her internship, she talked to as many staff members as she could. And by watching and listening and asking questions, she narrowed down her interest in the field. "In addition to doing the tasks I was assigned, I made my own opportunities," Ana says. "I asked a lot of questions. I went up to certain writers and reporters and asked to shadow them, so I could see what they did. I went the extra mile, and I learned along the way." Thoughts of law school and plowing through contract negotiations went flying out the window. TV work was what she wanted to do, perhaps in the area of press relations.

To solidify her interest in the field, Ana did a second internship the following summer, this one at KNBC-TV, now NBC 4, in Los Angeles. Again, the position was unpaid, but because she already had experience, this time she was able to take on a lot more responsibility. She also learned a great deal more. She continued to find out about the many jobs associated with television work. And she was shown how to research stories, how to interview, and what was involved in producing. This is when she decided that TV production was her real passion. It was very hands-on, very in the moment, and very exciting. In fact, the whole internship was so exciting and she did such a great job that her supervisor asked her to stay on, which she did for the fall quarter.

Ana's next internship was actually in a completely different field. In addition to her newfound love of TV production, she had always had a great interest in politics. For more experience and to extend her horizons a bit, she did an internship with a local congressperson through a history of Los Angeles class she was taking at college (she was a history major). Through that internship, she met a huge number of interesting people and learned a lot about the ins and outs of local politicking— important knowledge for many different careers as well as incentive to keep up her non-career-related involvement in politics.

During the last quarter of her senior year, Ana did her final internship, in Washington, D.C. This one combined her personal passion for politics with her career interest in news and entertainment: She interned in the News Summary Office of the White House Press Office. There her responsibilities were to find and copy articles that showed what the various news agencies were saying about the administration and the different slants they took on the president's activities. She attended press conferences held in the West Wing by the press secretary, was briefed on what the president was doing, and then went back to her office to go through hundreds of newspapers and clip out articles that related to the president's work.

Ana loved both living in Washington and having the chance to be part of a political hub like the White House. But some parts of her job were less than thrilling—in fact, some of it was a grind. She hadn't known she'd have to go through more than three hundred newspapers every day to search out articles that tied in to the presidency. So, as she did during her TV station internship, she made her own opportunities. She went to her boss and asked if she could compile the articles as well as clip and copy them. He said yes and said she could also help him write up the literature relating to the clippings. Then she asked, "In addition to clipping and copying and compiling, what else can I do?" Her boss, who was very supportive, told her to be pro-active, to start tracking down events that interested her, and to let him know what they were.

Ana jumped right on it. She started befriending people in different offices throughout the complex to find out what was happening. Quickly, she learned about ceremonies that would take place on the South Lawn and in the Rose Garden, and thought that one in the Rose Garden would be especially exciting to attend. So she went to her boss again and pitched the idea to him—if I get all my work done on this day, she said, would you arrange for me to attend the ceremony? He said, "Absolutely."

Then he pitched an idea to her. He told her that the president was going to be flying into Washington on *Air Force One* on the weekend and that staffers were needed to be there to greet him. He said that even though her internship followed a Monday through Friday schedule, that the hours would be in addition to her forty-hour week, and that she wouldn't be paid, it would be a great opportunity for her to be part of history—and it would help out the people arranging for the president's greeting. Would she be interested? Ana said, "Absolutely."

Because she took the initiative and made the most of her internship time, Ana now has great photos, and great memories, of the president and several Russian leaders landing in a helicopter on the White House lawn. By seeking out extra responsibility, and getting up the nerve to ask, she was able to experience a number of events most people never get to see. She also improved her work situation and met people from all walks of life, many of whom are still contacts, throughout the White House staff.

Ana says that she was lucky that her boss was so supportive; some supervisors aren't as encouraging. But you won't know what additional responsibilities or what unique events or opportunities are possible unless you ask.

When her internship ended, Ana received the best compliment—she was offered a full-time position at the News Summary Office. But though she had enjoyed the experience and her time in Washington, she was graduating, and knew that TV production was what she wanted to do. In fact, she had already been accepted into a master's program in television production and left to begin school.

But Ana had also made the most of the many student services at UCLA. She had attended a job fair there months before and had talked in depth with a representative from a Los Angeles TV station about her great interest in TV production. Two weeks after her master's program started, Ana received a call from the woman, who offered her an entry-level staff position at the station—in the number two TV market in the country! After talking with several of her professors, who told her she'd get more hands-on experience than she would ever get in school and that she'd be crazy not to take the job, Ana took it.

She's been moving upward and onward ever since: from the entry-level production-assistant position to freelancing for a number of TV stations (including NBC, Fox, Univision, and Telemundo) to her current job with the talk show, where she began as a post-production coordinator and was recently promoted to associate director.

Ana is now living her dream. And she believes her internships had everything to do with making that happen. "Internships teach you so much," she says, "and really give you the competitive edge for getting a great full-time job."

Her advice? "Work hard. Make yourself stand out by doing a better job than anyone else. And do more than you're asked, don't just do the minimum, go above and beyond. If you're always busy and enthusiastic, you'll definitely be noticed, and everyone will want you on his or her team—companies often hire from within, and they'd rather hire someone who they already know works hard and has the talent."

Another big must: Don't burn any bridges. "Especially in the entertainment field, everyone is related to everyone else. If you bad-mouth someone, her sister or her kid or her colleague is probably standing right behind you. And don't look down on someone younger than yourself. A woman who interned at the TV station where I had my first job is now a well-respected producer and might be my boss some day."

Two final "do's": Do work your network and do be persistent—during your internship and on your way up the ladder. For five months before she was hired by the talk show, Ana called and called the production company looking for a position; she didn't know anyone on the show, but she did keep up with a former colleague who knew the executive producer. But even though she kept calling, she didn't get anywhere. The person she talked to told her that they were all staffed up, that the new producer had brought in her own people.

But suddenly there was an opening, and her contact got right in touch with Ana: she had the credentials—could she start in a few days? She could! Her initiative and her expertise won her the job, and she's now happily following both her career path and her calling.

Chapter 3

Choose the Right Kind of Internship

Once you've gotten an idea of where your greatest interests lie and the skills you have or would like to develop, the next thing to do is consider the kind of internship you'd like to do— and when, where, and for how long you'd like to do it. All internships are meant to be learning experiences, where you can explore and experiment and grow and pursue interests, but one size doesn't fit all. We'll talk more in Chapter 6 about how to choose the best internship to suit your goals and wishes and personality, but now let's take a look at the kinds of internships and related options that are available.

Summer Internships

While many high school, college, and graduate students do an internship during some part of the academic year, most students prefer to do them in summer, because they have more time to devote to the experience (unless, of course, they're taking classes as well). A good number of summer internships are forty-hour-per-week positions and run for ten weeks (though they can be shorter or longer or part-time; it's up to the employer), so the summer break is usually an ideal time to fit one in. In addition, many employers think summer for their internship opportunities so that interns can help man their organizations while full-time employees go off on vacation, so you may have more choice if you decide to do an internship after the close of an academic year.

Summer interns also have the opportunity to have their position extended into the fall—often employers will be reluctant to give up the extra hands and brainpower or a project the intern was working on needs a bit more time to complete. Trina, a summer intern for a California assemblyman, stayed on through September and October because full-time staffers took vacation then while the legislature wasn't in session. Because her internship was in the same city where she went to college, she was able to continue part-time during the fall quarter and thus gained even more experience and insight during the extra months.

Another advantage of summer internships is that you can do one right after your freshman year. The earlier you can start doing internships the better, and with a year of school under your belt you may be ready (though we do recommend that most freshmen get some advice from their career center or internship office before committing to an internship). Lorena, who had been encouraged to do an internship by her older sister, who couldn't say enough about her own internship experience, jumped right on the application process at the start of her freshman year and lined up a great internship for the following summer. She got so much out of the program that she ended up doing four internships during college—starting early gave her the time. She was offered a full-time job after graduation in her final internship spot: the White House Press Office.

Summer internships, as well as internships at any other time of the year, can be paid or unpaid, at the discretion of the employer; there are no guidelines that dictate whether or not you have to be compensated. In the past, most internships were not paid; but, happily, now, more and more interns are being paid for the work they do. For example, a full-time summer intern at the *Washington Post* makes about $750 a week (it's still very unusual, though, for interns in the arts or the media to be compensated). Even if you aren't paid, you still can receive academic credit for a summer-long internship experience.

Winter-Term Internships

Another popular time to do internships, for those whose schools provide this opportunity, is during the winter term. A number of colleges throughout the country follow what's known as a "four-one-four" schedule in which students take classes for the first four months of the academic year, then have one month, usually January, to pursue intense independent study or an internship, and then complete the school year with four more months of regular class work (some colleges offer winter-term options that range from three to seven weeks). Students are often required to participate in at least three winter-term programs to graduate—some schools, such as Middlebury College, provide winter-term options only to sophomores, juniors, and seniors—and most designate a minimum number of hours that must be completed for credit.

Like summer programs, winter-term programs, sometimes called *fieldwork* programs, allow students to put full-time effort into self-discovery and experiential learning. Lowell, for example, a DePauw University student, spent one winter term interning in a nearby police department to learn the basics for a career with the FBI. The things he learned, he said, everything from what to look for when patrolling to how to book offenders, wasn't found in any textbook. And the experience, he was certain, would put him at the forefront when it came time to apply for a job.

Like DePauw University, Bennington College believes wholeheartedly in the benefits of the winter-term experience. Each year, the college requires all students to participate in an off-campus program in which they work or intern in a position that complements their area of study, from publishing to teaching to medicine to social work. By completing four different programs, students not only gain insight into their passions but develop networks and confidence that pave the way for real-world work.

Other schools that offer winter-term experiences include Oberlin, Colorado College, Gustavus Adolphus College, Macalester College, Mount Holyoke, Graceland University, and Franklin College. Hanover College, and several others, offer four-four-one programs in which students can study abroad, do independent study, or pursue an internship during the month-long spring term.

Academic-Year Internships

Though summer internships are more prevalent, plenty of students choose to do an internship during the academic year, particularly if it's an opportunity in or right near their college or university (school-year internships are generally more available in large cities). Usually these internships follow the local school's course system—either the quarter system or the semester system—but most follow the ten-week-long quarter system. However, the length of many internships is negotiable, so if you find one that sounds wonderful except that it doesn't fit your schedule, we encourage you to contact the company and try to negotiate a more suitable time frame.

If you want to concentrate on your internship alone, instead of doing one in addition to taking several classes, you can arrange to take the quarter or semester off (see pages 30 and 41 for more on what to do to get credit and how to take the quarter or semester off). But many students choose to do an internship along with their coursework, so they don't fall behind in credits and take longer to graduate. If you decide to try one during the fall, winter, or spring quarter along with one or more classes, we encourage you to negotiate a schedule that limits your internship hours to no more than ten or twelve a week. Why so few? Because, while you're in school, your main job is to learn from your professors and your studies. Yes, your internship will be a learning experience, but it's an adjunct to your classes, and shouldn't be the focus of your university years. Devoting too much time to an internship during the school year can negatively affect your GPA—not to mention your sanity.

Some students, of course, are able to handle a heavy class load in addition to many internship hours. If you're incredibly energetic and can manage your time well, you can probably do it. If you're a graduating senior and have already completed a lot of your credits, it may be possible to handle more internship hours too. But many students feel overloaded trying to do both, so if you think you'll be stressed, try to keep your internship to just a few hours a week. If you also hold a part-time job, the way many students do, you would be wise to limit your internship hours even more. You'll still get a lot from the experience, but you won't exhaust yourself along the way. If an internship seems perfect except for the number of hours required, take the initiative and talk to the employer, who might turn out to be flexible.

Like the summer intern who's asked to stay on into the fall, a school-year intern may also be asked to stay longer, sometimes for

TAKING THE QUARTER OR SEMESTER OFF

If you decide to do a school-year internship and want to concentrate just on it, rather than fit it in with classes, you'll need to arrange to take the quarter or semester off. At UCLA, undergraduate students who take only one quarter off are still considered registered students and just need to notify the registrar that they won't be taking classes. Students who take two or more consecutive quarters off must reapply for admission by going to the registrar's office and filling out an application for readmission. Most likely your college or university has a similar process, but check with your department head and the registrar for complete information.

the entire year. Employers often want interns to continue to work with them to get a better look at the intern's possibilities for a full-time position after graduation—very helpful to them, and a major plus for you.

Full-Year Internships

While the typical internship runs for ten weeks and some run for a semester, a number of internships are set up to last through the academic year. One agency that offers full-year internships is the Los Angeles Passport Agency. Students are taken on part-time for all three quarters, giving the interns extensive experience and the managers and staff a great look at the interns' hiring potential. If students successfully complete the internship during their sophomore or junior year, they are sometimes offered continuing year-long internships through to graduation. When they graduate, like Mark, who worked at the Passport Agency for two years, they might even be offered a full-time career position with the office.

Co-Op Programs

Co-ops programs, which are formally known as *cooperative-education programs,* have been in existence for many years. They're very much like standard internships, in that you spend time employed in a professional work environment and try the field on for size, but there are also several differences.

One big difference is that, although internships can be either paid or unpaid, co-op assignments are always paid. Like regular employees, students are paid by their employer for the work they do, helping make school more affordable while they learn new skills.

Another big difference is the length of time involved. While the typical internship runs for ten weeks, a typical co-op internship alternates six months in school with six months on the job. The longer period on the job gives employers a better chance to meet their staffing needs, to train students, and to determine students' potential. It gives students an extended opportunity to explore a possible career.

Another difference is that, while internships don't need to be related to your major but can be in any field you want to check out, co-op situations are usually related to the student's academic studies and offer academic credit in that area.

Just like internships, co-op programs are a great way to get on-the-job training and experience, the opportunity to grow and learn, and a huge edge when it comes time to look for a full-time job.

Volunteer, Study, Work, Intern, or Teach Abroad

In addition to many opportunities in your home town or state and across the United States, there are also many programs that let you intern—or study or work or volunteer or teach—in a foreign country. Some of these programs may have a language requirement, and traveling to certain countries may have additional requirements; but if you're looking for travel adventure, a new cultural experience, a chance to nurture your independent spirit, and a great place to learn and spread your wings, a program abroad may be just the thing for you. Spending time in a foreign country can give you insight not only into yourself but into people from very different walks of life and can help you share and develop views on everything from politics to philosophy to music to—that wonderful essential—food!

Roberta had a life-changing experience in Ghana, where she worked as an HIV/AIDS educator. She not only helped deliver and resuscitate a breach baby, but she saw firsthand how Ghanaian people often desert those with advanced AIDS, even members of their own family. Her volunteer-abroad program gave her a unique opportunity to understand how social dictates and religious beliefs can affect a nation's health. It also helped her decide on her career direction—she plans to go to medical school and return to Ghana when she graduates to open a family clinic.

Volunteer- and Study-Abroad Programs

Volunteer and study positions, of course, will not be paid, but it's also important to know that fees may be associated with both: Many programs require that you pay your own airfare and living expenses, while some may provide housing but ask you to pay for meals. Study-abroad programs will also have tuition requirements. For example, Syracuse University's study-abroad program, with locations in London, Madrid, Strasbourg, Florence, Hong Kong, and Singapore, has a semester fee of $6,000 to $8,000, but this includes travel expenses, housing, and some meals; students must also pay $13,000 in tuition. The International Studies Abroad program, which primarily runs study-abroad programs but also volunteer programs in Mexico, Costa Rica, Chile, and Argentina, has fees ranging from $2,200 to $5,500. When considering these kinds of programs, it's important to review all your options and choose the one that's right for you. Different programs that offer opportunities in the same city could provide you with entirely different experiences.

As far as length of stay goes, study-abroad opportunities generally last for a semester (if you're on the quarter system, you may have to drop out for two quarters and re-register when you return to school, an easy process; see p. 30), but they can run from one week to the whole summer to a year-long opportunity. Volunteer positions will vary by program. Some, like the Peace Corps, require a two-year commitment and also require that applicants have already received their B.A. or B.S. degree.

Work-Abroad Programs

Work-abroad positions are generally three to six months in length (although longer openings are available for those looking for full-time jobs), and many are offered in the summer. Some are paid, and some are not. For example, the British Universities North America Club (BUNAC), a non-profit organization, assists students in finding paid work for up to six months in Great Britain and Canada, up to four months in Ireland and Australia, and up to one year in New Zealand. Fees range between $205 and $550, depending on location. Other short-term work-abroad opportunities are available in a number of countries around the globe.

Most work-abroad programs will either provide you with or help you obtain a work permit. It's almost impossible now to get legal permission to work overseas, but many countries have established work programs just for college students and recent graduates and provide temporary, short-term work permits for people in these programs. Many work-abroad programs also help you find housing, offer workshops, or provide tips on living and working abroad as well as travel and cultural opportunities. To work abroad you need to be fluent in the language of the country you'll be staying in.

Intern-Abroad Programs

Internships in foreign countries run the gamut of interests, from business to banking to communications to science to agriculture to arts to engineering to hotel management—to just about anything you can think of. They also are available in many parts of the world, though current security issues have reduced or eliminated them in some regions, including the Middle East. If you'd like to consider an internship abroad, but have security concerns, a good organization to check out is the U.S. Department of State, which offers internships in embassies and consulates around the world. You can also get an international experience right in the United States by doing an internship through the U.S. Mission to the United Nations, which has internship openings in Washington, D.C., as well as in various cities across the country, and through other international organizations with U.S. operations.

Like internships in the United States, internships in foreign countries can be paid (though generally very little) or unpaid. And like study- and work-abroad programs, many international internships have fees associated with them. Fees depend on the organization, the internship location, and the length of stay, but they can run from a few hundred dollars to several thousand. Arcadia University, for example, places interns in London, Edinburgh, Sydney, and Canberra at a fall or spring semester cost of $12,000 (which includes housing, tuition, breakfasts, and insurance). Other organizations that place interns internationally include AIESEC, a student-run international group that offers business-related internships in many countries (www.aiesecus.org); CDS, which runs programs in Germany, Argentina, and Turkey in business and technical fields (www.cdsintl.org); and the American-Scandinavian Foundation, which provides placements in Scandinavian countries (www.amscan.org). Other international organizations and their Web sites are listed on the CD that accompanies this book. You can also browse the "international internship" pages of colleges and universities' Web sites to learn about programs for nonenrolled students.

Teach-Abroad Programs

Teaching abroad is another great way to learn about another culture as well as about yourself. However, unlike other living-abroad options, which are open to both undergrads and those who have obtained their degree, a bachelor's degree is a prerequisite for most teaching positions overseas. Your chance of securing a great position is also enhanced if you have a TEFL teaching certificate. *TEFL* stands for Teaching English as a Foreign Language and is also sometimes known as *TESOL*, for Teaching English to Speakers of Other Languages, or *ELT*, for English Language Teaching (see p. 72 for information on how to get a TEFL certificate). TEFL training will give you teaching opportunities in addition to those available with a B.A. as well as open the doors to higher-paying jobs. Having a K–12 teaching certificate will also give you the option of teaching at international and bilingual schools overseas; for example, teaching at schools attended by children of U.S. diplomats stationed in other countries. If you have a Ph.D., you may be able to do university-level teaching. All teaching positions require that you have excellent command of the English language, and some require a certain level of fluency in the host country's language.

Teaching positions abroad are generally paid positions, and the salaries are usually large enough to cover typical living costs. The Japanese Exchange and Teaching (JET) program, for example, pays participants approximately $32,000 a year, and host institutions help with finding reasonably priced housing; other programs provide subsidized living quarters, though you will probably need to pay your airfare. Teachers usually sign a one-year contract, which some organizations make renewable for one or two additional terms. Work visas are generally included as part of signing on with a program, and some groups also provide paid training as well as opportunities for cultural exchanges—which, of course, you'll have right in your classroom and which will help you learn and grow just as your students will learn and grow from interacting with you. Teaching positions are available in schools throughout the world and at schools for children of foreign-based U.S. government employees run by the Department of State.

If you haven't traveled outside the United States before or you'd like some insight into the country where you'll be teaching or studying or working or volunteering, it's a good idea to get some pointers on how to travel to and live in the new place you'll soon be calling home—being a savvy, safe, and respectful global citizen is an important part of the travel experience. For tips on how to make the most of your time abroad, check your study-abroad office center for travel workshops and other information sessions, and Chapter 6 for more resources as well as some dos and don'ts.

For tips on funding trips abroad, see Chapter 6 and the accompanying CD.

One Student's Experiences with Programs Abroad

Siri Somporn decided to do her first internship because she wanted to improve her Spanish. As an international development major (an interdisciplinary course of study that focuses on developing countries) she knew that being fluent in Spanish would be particularly helpful to her future career, which she thought would focus on government service, perhaps as a senator. She also wanted to experience another culture and interact with native Spanish speakers on a daily basis.

An internship in Central or South America seemed like the ideal situation.

Siri began researching possibilities not far into her freshman year. She spent a lot of time online, and discovered the BUNAC site, which provides information on how the non-profit helps students find short-term paid jobs in Great Britain, Canada, and Asia. Though the organization didn't cover Latin America, the information gave Siri insight into living and working in a foreign country.

From there Siri launched out on her own. After doing more research to see what programs were available for Central America, she also contacted alumni who had interned or worked there. She decided what she wanted to do was teach English in Costa Rica, but she also decided that she wanted to find a position there herself. At the end of her freshman year, she left—without a job lined up—to spend the summer there.

With the information she had gathered guiding her and knowing she could hook up with one of the study-abroad or volunteer-abroad programs she had learned about if she couldn't find work, Siri found a job tutoring English in a private high school. Twice a week she helped students with their homework and their language skills. The job paid only minimally, but Siri kept down her costs by staying with family friends who lived there.

"For all of my internships, and I ended up doing a lot of them, an important part of my choice criteria was finding an internship in a city where I knew people and could stay with them," Siri says. "By not paying any rent, or paying only a small amount, I was able to live on very little, which made many more experiences possible."

Teaching was a great way to immerse herself in the culture. By working with kids, she used and improved her Spanish. And by tutoring only two days a week, she had plenty of time to travel and learn about the country. "Whether you want to be a teacher or not, teaching English is a perfect start for anyone with international interests,"

Siri explains. "You meet all kinds of people and get a good sense of what life is like there. And it's a good foot in the door—the contacts you make can help you find office work or further your career later."

But her job was fairly difficult at first and not exactly what she expected. She had thought she would be given lesson plans and complete instructions on how to assist the regular teacher. But when she started, the school administrator pretty much said, here are the students, and please go ahead and teach them.

Luckily, because she had talked to alums who had taught in similar situations, Siri had known that finding resources in a foreign country can often be daunting. So she had brought a lot of books with her, including a dictionary and several workbooks. She was able to put some worksheets together and went on from there. "Be prepared when you teach abroad," she advises future teachers. She also recommends making copies of the materials you bring to leave as a gift to your school.

Siri's second internship was much briefer: a three-day work experience during her sophomore year for the U.S. Department of Agriculture. Again, Siri decided to take the position so she could use and improve her Spanish skills. She worked at a trade show in Chicago that was held to encourage exporting, and translated information for prospective buyers from Spanish-speaking countries. While the job wasn't a paid position, her travel and hotel expenses were covered. Siri was able to meet businesspeople from many parts of the world and have an international experience in the heart of the United States.

Siri's third internship tied into the first. While she had originally thought she might be a politician, her work in Costa Rica had opened her eyes to a new possibility: a career in education. With teaching experience on her résumé, Siri applied for and won a very competitive internship in the public affairs office of the U.S. Department of Education, in Washington, D.C. Once again, the internship was unpaid, but this time Siri was awarded a $1,000 college-funded scholarship. And once again she saved money by staying with family friends.

As an intern in the public affairs office, Siri's main responsibility was to answer education-related inquiries. Some of her favorites were letters from students asking for raises for their teachers! But in addition to letter writing, Siri was also able to attend White House press conferences and talk to speechwriters for the Secretary of Education. And she took part in research for the National Commission for the High School Senior Year. Through everything she did, she gained great insight into government-level education operations and saw firsthand what it was like to live in the nation's capital.

During her junior year, Siri continued to pursue her interest in education, but this time through two study-abroad programs, one to Cuba and one to Chile. In Cuba, she did a semester of anthropological research that was related to Cuba's Chinese community (she minored in anthropology, and the research position developed through a class she took). In Chile, she interned for nine months with Amnesty International.

Here again, Siri designed her own internship. She knew she wanted to go to Latin America and began to research the possibilities. When Amnesty International turned up and intrigued her, she contacted the organization and basically asked what she could do for them. They told her that an international criminal court was being ratified in Chile and that she could go there to research and write a paper about the ratification process. She found a professor who would sponsor the research as independent study and went directly from Cuba to Chile.

Her time there was incredibly exciting. She developed a large network of contacts, and because of her language proficiency, she was able to interview people involved with expanding and protecting human rights. It was also difficult, because there was no formal program. But since there was no formal program, she could be independent and make her experience what she wanted it to be.

Not one to waste an opportunity, Siri spent the summer after her fourth year (she took five years to complete her B.A.) interning at the American Citizen Services, a division of the U.S. State Department, in the U.S. Embassy in Bangkok, Thailand. She had applied earlier to intern at the embassy in Venezuela, for another chance to use and improve her Spanish skills, but her security clearance had gotten lost and she hadn't been able to go. "Always follow up once you send in an application," Siri advises. "The second time around, I was more vigilant. And leave plenty of time to get security clearance. Getting a State Department internship is one thing. Getting security clearance is another. It's a very detailed interview, and then interns are low on the list for getting their clearance processed. Mine took six months, which is actually on the short side. I left for Bangkok only two days after I received clearance."

Once there, Siri helped U.S. citizens in Thailand in a variety of ways: to renew their passports, deal with tax and Social Security issues, get a Thai driver's license, locate missing colleagues or relatives, and visit U.S. citizens in jail. She attended the trials of U.S. citizens and created the *Prisoner's Informational Pamphlet,* which detailed the Thai judicial system, the rights of prisoners, and the role the U.S. Embassy played in Thailand. All of her previous internship efforts put her in a position to take on real responsibility there and made her time in Thailand a rewarding experience. This internship was even paid, and she was provided with a fully furnished apartment.

"I'd say this was the most beneficial internship," Siri says. "I really learned a lot. And at that point I was considering going into foreign service, so the contacts I made were invaluable. I'd suggest interns always keep any business cards they're given—you never know when they'll come in handy. And I'd also recommend always getting a letter of recommendation from your supervisor at the end of your internship program."

After completing her stay in Thailand, Siri's incredible passion to see the world and fashion her own future continued. She interned again with the State Department, this time in Los Angeles at the Office of Foreign Missions, providing support services to the diplomatic community in the Southwest. And then she studied abroad for two quarters, at the University of Natal, in Durban, South Africa, as well as volunteered with Habitat for Humanity, helping build houses.

GETTING CREDIT

Though some colleges and universities require that you be at a certain level, such as a junior or senior, to receive credit for an internship, it's possible to get credit for just about any internship that's offered. It's up to you, though, to arrange for it. To receive credit, you need to find a professor who's willing to sponsor you. If you can't find one on your own, most colleges have departments or centers, like UCLA's Center for Community Learning, that will help you do so.

So what is she doing now, after so much travel and so much exploration? Today Siri is the marketing coordinator for the Latin American market for the Tourism Authority of Thailand, working in their Los Angeles office. She helps promote tourism in Thailand and uses her language skills to translate from Spanish to Thai—she's now also fluent in Thai. Her internship in Bangkok enabled her to get this position. And her internships relating to education and her study abroad helped her get the job she's about to start: a "dream job" working for Arcadia University recruiting students to study abroad. "This position usually requires a master's degree, which I don't have," Siri says. "But because I had so much relevant experience, I was able to convince them to interview me. And once I got my foot in the door, I got the job."

Fellowships

Fellowships are a little-known form, and possibly a misunderstood form, of internships. A fellowship—following in the footsteps of the original definition, which is an association of people with common beliefs and interests—is a paid position, usually for one to two years, though it can be as short as six months, in which you can develop advanced skills before taking a full-time job in your chosen field. Rather than a career position, it's an opportunity to really immerse yourself in the kind of work you plan to do and gain additional expertise and experience. Fellowships are usually offered through universities, foundations, government agencies, and other organizations, and most require that you have already completed your undergraduate degree; many are available only to graduate- or doctoral-level students.

Fellowships are an important way for employers to check out top potential hires, so doing a fellowship can be a direct route to landing a job with the organization. For example, the U.S. State Department runs the Foreign Affairs Fellowship Program, in which they take on men on women who are interested in foreign service careers. The program recruits applicants interested in such things as international affairs, political and economic analysis, and administration and then places them in positions in which they can develop skills that are needed to work for the State Department. At the completion of their fellowships, the students have great real-world experience and training, and the State Department has an immediate source of talented, proven staff.

Fellowship positions are generally full-time and the pay can be comparable to a full-time career position, up to $40,000 or more a year, though most are at a lower level. You can find fellowships in virtually every field, from the American Symphony Orchestra League's Orchestra Management Fellowship Program (designed to launch careers in orchestra management) to the California Sea Grant State Fellow Program (an excellent opportunity for graduate students deeply interested in marine resources). See Chapter 4 and the accompanying CD for additional information on fellowships and fellowship opportunities.

Research Opportunities

Research opportunities are also great ways to really delve into an area of interest. Available in various areas of science, most research positions are generally geared toward post-graduate students, though some are open to graduate and undergraduate students too. For example, a think tank like the Rand Corporation generally looks for someone with an advanced degree to do in-depth research in a field the organization is concentrating on—say, security or the situation in Iraq. They may also have openings available if you need a project on which to base your graduate or doctoral thesis. Undergraduate opportunities are often available through your college or university. At UCLA, a program called the Student Research Project enables undergrads in the liberal arts and sciences to work with an appropriate professor for a quarter; other schools offer similar programs, and your college may have one as well. Three such schools are the University of Pennsylvania (www.dept.physics.upenn.edu/undergraduate/lablist. html#lamont), the California Institute of Technology (www-unix .mcs.anl.gov/mathmodeling/resoptu.html lists their program and the Web sites of many other programs), and the University of Oregon (www.biology/uoregon/SPUR). In addition to the research positions available on your home campus or across the United States, there are also a good number of opportunities abroad.

Many research positions are full-time and paid, and can last from a few months to a full year; however, a good number are also part-time and unpaid. Whichever type you choose, it can be a wonderful way to network with colleagues with similar interests, confirm your career direction, broaden your expertise and your experience, and open doors to an exciting position in your chosen field.

Language Programs

While you might not think of attending a language school as an internship option, spending time improving your language skills or learning a second, or third, language can be a great way to make yourself more attractive to employers. It's also a wonderful opportunity to explore another world and learn a lot about yourself. A language school experience, particularly one in a foreign country, is an excellent way to jump-start your career and discover your passions.

TEN TOP LANGUAGE SCHOOLS

- Spain: Don Quijote (www.donquijote.org)

- Italy: Lorenzo de' Medici Institute of Florence (www.lorenzodemedici.it)

- Germany: Goethe-Institut (www.goethe.de)

- Japan: KCP International Language Institute (www.kcpinternational. com)

- France: École France Langue (www.france-langue.fr)

- Hungary: Languages Abroad (www.languagesabroad.com)

- Portugal: CIAL Centro de Linguas (www.cial.pt)

- Sweden: Eurolingua Institute (www.eurolingua.com)

- Russia: Liden & Denz (www.lidenz.ru)

- Worldwide: EF International Language Schools (www.ef.com)

A particularly appealing part of language schools is their great flexibility: programs are usually available at any time of the year, and many have flexible course periods, so you don't have to make a big time commitment up front. Say, for example, you decide to take a two-week intensive course at a school in Mexico, to spiff up your Spanish because you're thinking of a career in which translation skills will be a plus. When the two weeks of six-hours-a-day study are up, you've learned a lot, but you'd like to stay on to learn more—not to mention that you haven't had much time to travel and immerse yourself in the culture. Because most language schools are private institutes and don't tie in to a college or university schedule, you can sign up for another two weeks or a month or six weeks on the spot; you don't have to wait till the next semester or the next summer to further improve the way you *habla Español*.

Unlike true internships and fellowships, which sometimes have specific age or school year requirements (for example, you need to be a continuing undergrad to apply for a State Department internship or a current or recent graduate student to apply for the Art Institute of Chicago's Museum Education Fellowship), you can attend a language school program whenever it fits your schedule and whether you're an undergrad, a graduate student, or someone who's long out of school and looking to make a career change. You can also be a complete beginner or have a bit of language training or speak and read the language quite well—programs are available for all levels.

Although you probably won't be able to receive credit for attending a private language school, because they're usually not accredited, it's possible to receive credit for a program run by a U.S. or foreign university. Language school tuitions will vary by length of stay and school location, but often they're quite reasonable compared to semester study-abroad program tuitions. The fee for a two-week classroom program through La Escuela de Idiomas D'Amore, a school in Quepos, Costa Rica, is approximately $845 U.S. For two weeks of classes and a home stay, the cost is close to $1,000 U.S.

With such a wealth of opportunities, it's likely that at least one of these options will fit the time you have available as well as the goals you have for an internship experience. While some programs do have fees, don't let that stop you from checking out the possibilities. See the accompanying CD for scholarship and other funding sources.

Chapter 4
How Many and Which Internships to Apply For

If you've been putting in the time to do a thorough, creative internship search, you've probably come up with a number of promising possibilities. Your list may include several finds from your school's internship office, a local organization you belong to, the corporation where your parents' neighbor works, and the Internet. It's probably a nice, big list. But should you apply for all the positions? How can you be certain that each choice could be a winner?

The only way to answer those questions is to continue on with your research. While all your selections may sound great as they're described in each organization's informational materials, it's up to you to dig deeper for the facts that will help you decide. So take another breath and jump back in. The time you spend now will prevent you from wasting time and energy later on an application—and possibly even in the internship—in a position that's not remotely right for you.

Finding the Facts

Start out your new round of research by thoroughly checking out every potential employer on your list. You want to know everything about them: the products or services they provide, how long they've been in business, how long their internship or fellowship program has been in place, whether or not they're involved in lawsuits or business difficulties that could negatively affect their livelihood or the completion of your internship, if they're well regarded and involved in the community—everything you can think of that will give you a good picture of who they are and if you'd like to be associated with them. This kind of information will help you decide whether you'd like to apply for their opening, and, if you do, will give you a ready bank of facts for your application and/or your interview.

The Internet and the Library

How can you uncover this necessary information? The Internet is a great place to look. Career-oriented Web sites such as www.vault.com and www.careerbuilder.com and internship-specific sites such as www.wetfeet.com provide dozens of profiles of well-known companies. The organizations themselves, of course, will include "about us" information on their own sites, and though they'll give you only the positives, they're a good place to get a sense of the company's overall focus. Newspapers, too, will provide helpful information; business sections often include articles on a variety of organizations, and many newspapers and magazines print lists of their picks for the best one hundred companies to work for or companies on the move. You can also check with your local Better Business Bureau to see if complaints have been lodged against a particular community organization.

The library can also be a great source of information. Most public libraries carry current and past issues of business-oriented magazines, such as *Business Week* and *Money,* as well as weekly journals with strong business sections, such as *Newsweek, Time,* and *U.S. News & World Report.* Books are also available (often in the investment section) that provide in-depth information on hundreds and even thousands of organizations around the world. Your local librarian will be able to direct you to helpful resources.

Campus Presentations

Campus information sessions and presentations hosted by local business organizations are also a good way to gather information and ask questions in person. Check with your school's career center and watch the local newspaper to see if any of the employers you're interested in will be sending representatives to speak somewhere nearby. You might even be able to talk with the very person who will be interviewing and hiring interns.

Reading the Fine Print

As you check out potential employers, remember to not only look into the company as a whole but also think about the particular department or division you'd be working with. For example, you may have located an internship with the Walt Disney Company and think that would be a great place to intern, especially if you're an art or a film major. But check the listing closely—the internship might be in administration or public relations. While it's possible you could make contact with Disney artists or directors while working in public relations, it's also possible that you won't, which could not only be frustrating but keep you from reaching your internship goals. If you're not sure what a specific department does, check informational materials or speak to someone in the marketing or public relations department.

One other point: Some internships are for a particular agency or organization rather than for a specific position. For instance, a number of internships are available at the White House, and you can specify which one you'd like to be considered for, say, in the Press Office. But that doesn't guarantee that you'll be given that position if you're accepted. You might be placed in Correspondence and spend most of your time writing congratulations letters to seniors who have turned one hundred. Once you're placed, you can't change the assignment, so think hard about whether you'd be happy with any position you might end up in before deciding to apply.

Working Your Network

Books, Web sites, and newspapers are great information sources, but there's nothing like real live people to give you the lowdown on internship experiences. One of the best ways to uncover the truth about a particular organization's ethics and environment is to ask someone who's worked there.

Internship Office Connections

If you're a student, your internship office or career center may be able to connect you with a student who interned or is currently interning in the same position or company you're interested in, especially if it's a local employer. The school's alumni association should also be able to make similar connections, for students and alums alike. Alumni organizations may also have files of members holding full-time jobs with organizations you want to check out; these individuals can tell you what it's like to work there now, from culture to upcoming projects to community involvement.

Company Referrals

The companies themselves should be another source of contacts. If you know an internship program has been ongoing, ask the company for the names of several people who have filled the position—if they won't provide them, that should be an immediate red flag. Get in touch with as many current or former interns as you can.

When you talk to someone who's been there, don't hold back.

This is your chance to ask the big questions that will tell you what you want to know. What's the management like? Is it a fairly casual or more structured environment? Are you given real responsibility or it the position mostly busy work with no opportunity to learn? Are the people friendly and supportive or too busy to provide guidance or encouragement? What kinds of projects did you work on? What's typical office wear? Does the internship offer a positive experience? Be sure to ask the person if he or she would encourage others to intern there. While you probably won't know the person and won't know if the two of you would see things in a similar light, just hearing from someone who's done what you're thinking of doing will add an important dimension to your deliberations.

Interns' Evaluations

If you can't locate someone to talk to, there's still a way to hear about former interns' experiences. Most college internship centers ask students to evaluate their experiences as interns, anonymously if they want, and those down-to-earth reviews are kept on hand for others to read through. Check your center's files as well as its Web site for great information from those truly in the know.

Mario, for example, landed an internship with a major motion picture company in New York City, an exciting-sounding opportunity for a film major. But though the position had been described quite differently, Mario ended up spending most of his time making coffee and doing errands for a director. It wasn't at all the learning experience he had expected, and he advised those interested in the position to save themselves the time and disappointment. His frank evaluation, posted on his university's Web site, prevented other students from having an equally unfortunate experience.

Kendra, on the other hand, found confirmation in evaluations she read about a State Department internship. After doing her own research, she thought it sounded like a perfect fit, and the glowing reports from students who'd held the position in the past gave her the confidence to send in her own application.

Searching Out the Supervisor

Another way to gather helpful information is to talk to the person who will be supervising the internship. Once you apply for the position, especially if it's for a local opening, you may be able to have your questions answered in an interview. But to find out some basic facts before you send in an application, you can arrange to talk to the supervisor by phone. If his or her name isn't provided in the listing, you may have to sleuth around a bit to find the right person. But all supervisors should be ready and willing to spend a few minutes answering specific questions; just make sure you have a well-thought-out list on hand so no one's time is wasted. While you talk, you may also be able to get a sense of whether or not you could work well with the person and if it sounds like interns in the department are just a cheap source of labor or are given true responsibility and opportunities to learn.

Meeting Your Individual Needs

Once you've gathered as much hard information as you can, start thinking about your internship choices from a personal perspective. Here are some important points to consider:

Does it Suit Your Interests, Talents, and Goals?

As you look through your possibilities, really think about the kind of work you'd be doing. An internship at the U.S. Department of Education might sound perfect if you think you want to go into teaching, but if you hope to learn about curriculum development, find out if that's something you'd actually do. Judy, a UCLA intern, hoped to learn about curriculum development in her education department position, but she found herself involved with work that had to do with policymaking. Another intern, Monica, from Harvard, thought she'd be able to further improve her language skills by working at the

Brazilian embassy, but her responsibilities never made use of her years of Portuguese classes. Try to find out if each internship position you're considering would make use of your skills and allow you to meet your goals. (If you haven't done it already, it might be a good idea now to list your goals to make sure the position will help you work toward them.)

Also make sure that each opening you apply for is in an area you really want to pursue. If you're a student, you might be majoring in a particular subject because your dad had the same major and expects you to go into the same field he's in, but your heart might not be in it. If you've been working for a few years, you might want to look at fellowships or live-abroad options in new career areas if you don't really enjoy your present job. Make sure each possibility is one that intrigues *you*. An internship should fulfill *your* dreams and goals, not meet a friend or family member's expectations.

Are You Considering the Opening for the Right Reasons?

Tran, a long-time skateboarder, came across an internship opening at a nearby skating magazine. He didn't really think he'd go into publishing or be involved in skateboarding for a career, but the thought of hanging out with pro skaters and being in a cool-sounding environment for the summer made him send in an application. He got the position—but was asked to leave a few weeks into the job. *He* had thought he'd have a fun summer, but *his supervisor* had thought Tran was going to help the staff through a heavy summer deadline schedule. Be sure any internship you apply for is in a field you really want to learn about and that can help you make career and life choices. Accepting an internship for the wrong reason—such as the following—is just a waste of everyone's time. "I've never really want to work there, but it sounds like it would be a good time for a couple of weeks," "I won't have to spend any time researching and interviewing, this alum I know said I could have the opening at her office," and "It's such a prestigious place to have on my résumé."

Is the Agency or Organization One You'd Like to Work in as a Full-Time Employee?

While doing an internship is a way to explore your options, many interns receive employment offers at the end of their ten or twelve weeks with the company—lots of employers think of an internship as a three-month-long job interview. Though you certainly don't need to accept a job offer and this doesn't have to be a key factor in your decision-making process, it's a good thing to keep in mind as you go through your choices. For example, if you're a senior who wants to go right to work after graduation and you know you'll need to live at home for a while until you have enough money for your own place, taking an internship in a city across the country might not be the best way to line up a great position to step right into.

Would You Be Comfortable Working There?

As you consider the possibilities, think of what the ideal environment would be. Would you rather work in a small office where you might have a better chance to interact with everyone, be given more responsibility, perhaps dress more casually, and maybe go through a more casual interview process? Or would you prefer a larger workplace, where you might get introduced to more facets of the business, have a larger choice of possible mentors, make more extensive contacts, and have a well-known business name to put on your résumé? Both situations have their pluses and minuses, so think about which is more likely to meet your needs.

Is the Internship Formalized or Less Structured?

The job description will let you know if the internship is structured or flexible. Read the information before deciding if it's the type of program you want. Often large corporations will offer a fairly formal program in which interns are introduced to several different departments, to give them an overall picture of how the company works and the many opportunities that are available. This can be a terrific way to check out a number of career options, but it also can be frustrating or nonproductive if you'd rather spend the entire internship learning about one particular field or job.

Is the Internship Paid or Unpaid?

If you had the choice, most likely you'd prefer the internship that pays you a salary or a stipend (a stipend is a lump-sum amount that you'd earn for the entire internship, for example, it might be $3,000 for a ten-week full-time position). The money would help with your living expenses and maybe even go toward longer-term dreams, such as graduate school or time off to travel. But if the internship sounds fantastic, even if it's not paid, you may want to see if you can do it anyway—it might be the chance of a lifetime to get involved in something special. To help with day-to-day costs, consider whether you could live at home or with friends, dip into savings, or get a scholarship or financial aid. While money is, of course, important, it's also extremely important to take advantage of exciting opportunities. And if an internship isn't paid, you might be able to negotiate a different benefit. Employers who offer unpaid internships are often a bit more flexible; for example, you might be able to ask for a specific responsibility or reduce the number of required hours to free you up for a part-time paid job. And you can arrange to do the internship for course credit.

Paid or not, you can still apply for funding to help you cover your costs. In fact, now is a good time to apply for financial aid, since it can sometimes takes months for a check to reach you. If you're already receiving financial aid, the good news is that it can be used for going abroad. If you're a student, check with your internship office for possible funding resources. A number of scholarship and other financing possibilities are also included on the accompanying CD.

Would You Be Happy Working in the Location?

Have you always wanted to travel through Europe? If you're an Easterner, would you like to see what the "left coast" is like? Does this seem like a good time to take a break from hectic big-city life? While you may have responsibilities or financial restrictions that limit your location choices (or circumstances that would keep you from accepting an internship extension in that area), matching where you'll do the internship to your goal of meeting new people and exploring new places will add another important dimension to the overall experience. Do keep in mind, though, related issues that may be important to you, such as weather, traffic, cost of living, environmental concerns, or difficulty finding housing.

Is It a Full-Time Program or Just a Few Hours a Week?

The internship you do needs to fit into your life and schedule. If you overload yourself with too much time on the job, your health, schoolwork, or day-to-day activities may suffer. If it won't put you behind in credits or negatively affect your finances, taking the summer or a quarter or semester off is a great way to fully immerse yourself in the experience. But you can also learn a lot in a much shorter period or in a long-term opening of ten or twelve hours a week. Choose internship programs that promise a challenging, exciting time, but don't do yourself in by taking on too much.

Do You Meet the Requirements?

When you read each description, carefully check that you have both the skills and the qualifications that the opening requires. For example, the description for an internship in a national park might read: "Candidates should have the ability to work independently; have strong office, oral communication, and organizational skills; and enjoy interacting with people. They must also have a valid driver's license, a personal interest in the field, and a willingness to work weekends." Even if you're the best organizer a supervisor could ever hope for, but you have a weekend job or don't drive, you shouldn't waste your time applying—your application simply won't make the cut.

Requirements can run the gamut from computer skills to writing skills (employers may want to see several writing samples) to leadership ability to having a particular major. Some will be age related or specify a certain education level. For instance, a travel grant might be available only for adventurers between the ages of seventeen and twenty-six, and a fellowship might be offered only to post-graduates. Some positions are open to all comers, though. For example, an internship at the Smithsonian Institution's Office of the Chief Technology Officer is open to high school students sixteen or older, recent high school graduates, college students, recent college graduates, graduate students, law students, career changers, and those re-entering the workforce.

A few internships and many of the positions abroad may have additional requirements. A study, work-, volunteer-, or teach-abroad situation might require a minimum level of language proficiency, a TEFL or TESL certificate (see page 72 for details), a minimum GPA, or a work permit (many international programs will make the arrangements for a permit or help you obtain one). If you apply for a State Department opening, you'll need to receive security clearance, which requires interviews and often several months to get.

Does the Job Description Light Your Fire?

When you think about the internship, do you imagine the possibilities? Do you want to send in your application immediately? Can you see yourself drinking it all in? Above all else, you want to apply for internships that you think will be enriching and that will give you the opportunity to tap into your passions.

Laurel, for example, a political science major at Syracuse, had experience working in local and statewide politics. But she was fascinated by international politics and knew that she wanted a career in

TEN TOP INTERNSHIP OPPORTUNITIES

- U. S. Department of State internships (www.careers.state.gov)

- The Japan Exchange and Teaching Program (JET) (www.mofa.go.jp/jet)

- Woodrow Wilson Center Internship Program (www.wwics.si.edu/index. cfm?fuseaction-opportunities.welcome)

- Department of Justice internships (www.usdoj.gov/careers/student_ programs.html)

- New Voices Foundation fellowship (www.newvoices.aed.org/home.html)

- Carnegie Endowment for Peace internships (www.carnegieendowment.org)

- New York City's Department of Citywide Administrative Services fellow-ships and programs (www.nyc.gov/internships)

- *Washington Post* internships (www.washpost.com/howardsimons)

- California Fellows Program (www.csus.edu/calst)

- The Peggy Guggenheim Collection Internship Program, Venice (www. guggenheim-venice.it/english/10_internship/01_internship.htm)

that world. When she learned about an internship at the Office of Legal, Legislative, and External Affairs, in the Office of the Inspector General in Washington, she applied on the spot. She was certain it was going to be an extraordinary experience—and it was. She came away from it, she said, "Yearning for more politics, more law, and more life in D.C."

Not every internship, though, will be an exciting, positive experi-ence; it's possible you won't enjoy it or that you'll discover the field is not for you. But you should start out with the belief that it will be ab-solutely great. Our advice is not to go for the just OK; we encourage you to go for the wow!

Making Your Final Picks

Once you've gathered all the information and checked that you meet the requirements, it's time to apply for the internships or other opportunities that sound most exciting. While it may take some time to complete the applications (see Chapter 8 for help with the process), we encourage you to apply to as many openings as you're interested in. Internships these days can be quite competitive, so by giving yourself several options you'll be much more likely to end up with a great situation. In addition, if you're offered several interviews, you'll get practice putting yourself out there and may even extend your network. And if you choose your candidates wisely, whichever offer you receive will be welcome.

Nate, a business economics major, applied to several large accounting and investment-banking firms in San Francisco after carefully researching all of them. He was asked by only one of them to come in for an interview, but because internship sounded like an exciting way to explore a possible career, he thought he'd be happy to work at the company after graduation, and the internship paid a stipend, so he was more than pleased to do the interview. And he was very happy to be selected for the opening.

Chapter 5
Possibilities through Networking

OK, you've made your decision—you want to do an internship. You realize it's the best way to really explore career possibilities and both discover and develop your skills and get the edge on landing a great job. Now to start hunting down some exciting internship choices.

When you start your search, remember to think big. Because internships have become so important, more and more companies and organizations have begun to offer them, and they're more diverse than ever before. So there are a lot of great possibilities out there, and it's very likely that a number of them will be right up your alley. But it's up to you to track them down. The best way to do that, and to make sure you don't miss out on any opportunities, is to keep a wide focus.

Say you're an undergrad with a major in English. You enjoy writing, and think you might want to go into teaching, so media-related and education internships might seem to be the only opportunities to check out. Well, you're right—looking for an internship in both of those areas is definitely a good idea. But why limit yourself to just those two fields? Many businesses and organizations need both writers and instructors, and by widening your search you might be able to find a challenging opportunity in a career area you never thought about before—one that can set you on a whole new, exciting course.

For example, Bernie, an English major, looked into a variety of openings at radio stations and TV stations because he thought he might be interested in going into some area of media work. But in addition to wanting to try a career possibility on for size, Bernie was also interested in seeing what it was like to live in a large metropolitan area, since he was from a small town and had never lived in a big city. He decided to see what the possibilities were through his school's Washington, D.C., internship program; by broadening his focus, he ended up doing an internship at the White House Press Office. There he not only was able develop his writing skills but also got a firsthand look at what life was like working in a government agency. He found out he enjoyed the stimulating atmosphere. He also experienced how much fun it was to live in D.C. In fact, it was so much fun that Bernie now plans to live there for at least a few years after graduation.

The same goes for other majors and other areas of interest. If you're a business major, financial-services opportunities are certainly one area to mine. But you can also think wider. Other private-sector businesses employ CPAs and marketing staff, from media and entertainment corporations to department stores to education outfits. Government offices do likewise; you might find a great accounting internship in the U.S. Department of Agriculture, where you could enrich your interest in health and natural resources while you see if an accounting career is what you thought it might be. If you're a computer science major, you could work for a technology company, but one with international connections in which you could learn about trade and export policy as well as expand your skills. You can even look into areas that have nothing to do with your major but that have always sparked your interest or just suddenly seem like something you'd like to try. By thinking outside the box and not limiting yourself to traditional roles or expected steps, you can add a whole new dimension to your internship experience.

The same goes for location. If you plan to do an internship during the academic year, your search will logically concentrate on areas close by your school, unless you plan to take the entire quarter or semester off. But if you do want to take time off or you plan to do an internship in the summer, there needn't be any geographic limits to your internship search. As you think about the where, we encourage you to think big—in fact, we encourage you to think globally. If you're from a small town, like Bernie, why not try out city life? If you've never traveled outside your state, why not see what another part of the country or the world is like? In addition to having a great career-defining experience, you could also have a great life-enhancing experience, and what could be better than that!

What are *your* interests? What would *you* like to explore? Which new part of the world would *you* like to spend some time in? As you look into all the wonderful possibilities that are available, keep your mind open, and don't hold yourself back. There's more out there than you may realize. And now is the time to find out if it's for you.

Taking the First Step

To begin your internship search, don't head for the nearest computer or your university's internship files. Take some time to do a little thinking before you jump in. Which career directions have you thought about already? What do you feel are your skills and interests or which skills did assessment tests define? (See Chapter 2 if you haven't taken advantage of these tests yet.) Which jobs do friends or relatives hold down that sound exciting or intriguing, even if they're outside your major or completely different from what you do now? Which areas of life—from entertainment to the environment to government issues to health to business—have always, or just recently, stirred your passions? Which careers have you always wondered about but never had the chance to look into? Which fields are likely candidates for someone with your major? Really dig in deep and consider all the possibilities. Then think, too, about where you'd like to do your internship. Do you need to stay close to home because of responsibilities or continuing schoolwork? Or can you look further afield, out of the area or even abroad? As you think, give yourself the freedom to fly. Nothing is too crazy. Everything is open to be explored.

Once you're got some ideas, consider adding to them by talking with a number of other people—career or internship counselors at your school, private counselors if you're no longer a student, friends, relatives, professors, people you work with, alums, anyone you think might have some good ideas about possible directions. By letting other people know you've started looking for an internship or other option, you'll not only get suggestions for a wide variety of areas to check out but possibly learn about actual opportunities as well. Some of the people you talk to may have internship programs through their organizations or they may know about interesting internship possibilities you may want to pursue.

Using School Resources

Internship Center Files and Web Sites

When you've got some promising directions in mind, set aside a chunk of time to work through your school's internship files. Your career center or internship office will likely have numerous listings of internship openings, and they're a great place to start compiling the positions you think you might want to apply for. Many offices will have opportunities broken down by local, national, and international locations, so remember to keep that wide focus and check into lots of possibilities—not only in different fields but in different parts of the country and the world.

Georgia, a human development major at the University of California at Davis, decided she wanted to take a quarter off and do an internship outside her small college town, in a large city. She also knew she wanted to intern in an area related to her major but wasn't sure exactly what. When she went to her school's internship center, not only did she find many file cabinets filled with information on internships in every imaginable field but she also found students working there who helped her discover openings that matched her interests. Counselors and advisors were also happy to help.

Career center and organization Web sites are other great places to look. The accompanying CD lists hundreds of Web sites for you to browse. You can also look at the Web sites of companies that appealed to you during your file-folder search. After reading through several drawers of folders, Georgia went on to browse the Web sites of organizations that sparked her interest. Many of the sites included application guidelines as well as job descriptions, so Georgia was able to determine right away if her qualifications matched the internship requirements. She ended up choosing and winning an internship in Washington, D.C., at the HeadsUp! Network arm of the National Head Start Association, which provides training and the latest research via satellite television to early-childhood educators.

When you check out your career center's listings, it's a good idea to check them frequently—we recommend looking every day. Not only will new listings arrive often, to be added to the cabinet files, but new postings will continue to show up online; e-mail makes it incredibly easy to send a listing to the career or internship office and it's also very simple to add an opening to an organization's Web site. By checking often, you won't miss out on any of the great opportunities, and you'll be able to get your application in on time if the position has an early deadline.

Career Center Books

In addition to listings of internship opportunities that organizations send directly to your college's internship program, your internship office or career center probably houses a number of books that detail thousands of current opportunities across the country and around the world. These books, such as *Internships 2005* and *The Internship Bible* by Mark Oldman, are updated annually and contain a comprehensive directory of internships and other options. Openings are listed by fields, such as finance and insurance; arts, entertainment, and recreation; and professional, scientific, and technical services, so paging through the different categories may lead you to new areas you'll want to look into.

Other Campus Departments, Schools, and Clubs

In addition to your career center or internship office, there are other places on campus where you can find out about available internships. Often companies will send notices of openings to particular academic departments. If they're looking for an intern with a background or interest in engineering, for example, they may just send the listing to the engineering department rather than the career center. Likewise, if a county prosecutor's office is looking for an intern, they might contact only a colleague or professor at the law school. So be sure to check with your academic-major office and with other departments and schools that might have listings of internships in an area you want to explore. If there are major-related clubs on your campus— for instance, an accounting club or a photography group—most likely members network with professionals in their field and may have some great leads for you to follow.

Campus Info Sessions

Local, national, and international businesses and organizations come to college campuses not only to recruit future employees but to provide information on internship opportunities. Your career center probably posts listings of when and where various companies will be making presentations, and by attending those of interest you can find out if they have an internship program. If you can't make the presentations because of classes or other conflicts, check with your career center later for brochures or handouts the company probably provided. Many organizations that can't make presentations will also send information and applications that the career center or internship office will be sure to make available.

Other Colleges and Universities

While your own institute of higher learning may offer internship, fellowship, and study- and work-abroad opportunities, so do hundreds of other colleges in most parts of the country. By checking out their Web sites or informational brochures, you can see the type of programs they offer and if any of them match your interests. The University of Rochester, for example, has internship opportunities in London, Berlin, Brussels, Paris, and Madrid in such fields as business, politics, theater, and museums. Syracuse University offers options in England, Spain, and Switzerland in areas including law, management, and public policy. Work and study programs related to African studies are available through the University of Pennsylvania. (See the accompanying CD for more college and university Web sites to browse.)

Using Nonschool Resources

If you're an undergrad or a graduate student, you've got numerous school-related resources at your disposal for tracking down terrific internships. But what if you've already graduated or have been working for several years? It's a good idea to tell friends and colleagues that you're actively searching for a fellowship, scholarship, volunteer, or live-abroad opportunity to explore new options or further develop skills. So talk it up, and follow all leads—it just might be the ticket to a more exciting career direction.

In addition to talking to people you know, there are a number of other ways to learn about promising positions.

Books, Web Sites, and Newspapers

While there are several books available that list internships, many of them focus on opportunities for undergrads and graduate students. But there are also a number of books that pinpoint possibilities for a wider range of ages. One of them, *The Back Door Guide to Short-Term Job Adventures,* by Michael Landes, covers all the bases. Another, *How to Live Your Dream of Volunteering Overseas,* by Joseph Collins and co-workers, concentrates on an important way to follow your passion while discovering new worlds. Your local library or bookstore will have many other books for you to look through, and a number are listed in the Appendix.

There are also a good number of Web sites that list internships and other options. Some are searchable databases of all kinds of internships, like www.wetfeet.com and www.internships.com, and some focus on particular opportunities, such as www.us.aiesec.org for business internship possibilities. You can also search job- and career-oriented sites such as www.vault.com and www.monstertrak.com for their pages on internships and related opportunities.

Another idea is to look for internships or fellowships by the city

---

TEN TOP WEB SITES FOR INTERNATIONAL OPPORTUNITIES

- **For volunteering abroad:** www.peacecorps.gov, www.interaction.org, www.globalroutes.org, www.vfp.org

- **For teaching abroad:** www.state.gov, www.iss.edu

- **For working abroad:** www.interexchange.org, www.ciee.org

- **For studying abroad:** www.gquest.org, www.arcadia.edu/cea

in which you'd like to do one. For example, if you want to explore what it's like to live in San Francisco, you can type the words *San Francisco* and *internships* into a search engine such as Google or Yahoo and see what turns up.

For an in-depth listing of a variety of Web sites, see the accompanying CD. And remember to check Web sites daily—new opportunities get posted all the time.

Newspapers are another great resource to search for interesting openings. Not only do many large-circulation papers (and their Web sites) have career-builder sections that list internships but they also often feature articles that profile companies and organizations, so you can see if a candidate is a company you'd be happy working with. The "Career Builder" section of the *Los Angeles Times* Web site (www.latimes.com) is a particularly valuable resource for ideas and opportunities. You can also check papers in your area as well as the Web sites for papers anywhere in the country.

Career Expos

Businesses and organizations make the college circuit to recruit promising students, but they also present information about themselves at town and city career expos. Often held at convention centers, career expos give a wide range of companies and agencies the chance to speak directly to students and graduates looking for work or for options such as volunteering. Many of these organizations also have active internship programs, so expos are a great way not only to learn about a company you're interested in but to find out about their internship program firsthand. Large-circulation newspapers often sponsor these kinds of expos, and local organizations such as the Chamber of Commerce and business groups get involved as well. Some of these sponsors, such as newspapers, often have internship programs of their own, so they're still another possibility to add to your search. To see if a career expo will take place in your area soon, check the business section of your local newspaper and the Web sites of associations that promote local business.

TEN TOP CAREER EXPOS

- Women for Hire (www.WomenforHire.com)

- JobFind (Boston) (www.careerex.com)

- Hire Diversity (www.hirediversity.com)

- Career Fairs (www.careerfair.com)

- National Job Fairs (www.nationaljobfairs.com)

- Tech Expo USA (www.techexpousa.com)

- Spring Break Career Expo (www.springbreakcareerexpo.com)

- Diversity Recruitment Career Fairs (www.eop.com/careerfair.html)

- Best Jobs USA (www.bestjobsusa.com/sections/can-careerfairs/index. asp)

- WorkSource (Washington State) (www.wa.gov/esd/work/events.htm)

Community, National, and International Organizations

It's not just companies and corporations that provide internship experiences. Clinics, laboratories, museums, interest groups, government agencies, social action groups, churches, environmental centers, schools—just about any organization you can think of is likely to have opportunities for interns. As you look for possibilities, keep in mind organizations you think do great work, say, the American Heart Association; organizations that you belong to or volunteer with, perhaps the YMCA or Habitat for Humanity; and organizations that you've heard of that just intrigue you, maybe a local agency that promotes AIDS awareness, a children's discovery center, or a business association. Some of the larger organizations may have speakers that make presentations to groups, but you can always contact them directly or get information from their Web sites. All of them are possible sources for exciting, life-directing experiences.

The Accompanying CD

This chapter (and others) provides lots of sources for your search, and the CD contains numerous Web sites you can start browsing immediately. The listings feature U.S. and international internships as well as volunteer, fellowship, and living-abroad opportunities. Just pop the CD into your computer to get started.

Getting Creative

If, after doing a lot of looking, none of the possibilities seems just right, you may need to try another tack—creating the opportunity yourself. There are a couple of ways you can do this.

If you're currently employed, the company you work for may have an internship program for students. While it may be a long shot, it's still worth talking to program administrators to see if there are openings for interns in a department that piques your interest. Say, for example, you work in administration but marketing is an area that you've been thinking might be more fulfilling. It's possible that you could continue to hold down your job part-time while doing the internship part-time. You'd continue to draw a salary while finding out if marketing is for you, and your employers would continue to benefit from your expertise as well as gain an intern who's already business savvy—a definite win–win situation. Making something like this happen will probably take some persuading on your part, but it's certainly worth a try if the opening seems to be just what you've been looking for.

If you're a student, it may be possible to design your own internship. Both internship offices and academic departments work hard to support students' interests, and some campuses have specific programs that help students come up with an internship idea, find a faculty sponsor, fund the experience, and make all the arrangements. This may take a lot of effort, but it may also give you the chance to tailor-make an opportunity. Chitra, a dance major, combined her love of travel and her interest in folk dancing by locating a community resource center in Mexico where she taught dance and studied traditional Mexican dance for six weeks during the summer. To make this dream internship a reality, she found the center, wrote a proposal, took it to the theater arts department and several other student offices, and eventually got the project funded through her university's College of Arts and Sciences. Though it took time and energy to put it all together, Chitra's customized internship enabled her to follow her passion and confirm that she was heading down the right career path.

Another strategy that's open to both students and nonstudents is to encourage an interesting company that doesn't offer an internship program to set one up—and take you on as the first intern. Say, when you're doing your search, you come across a great-sounding organization that you'd really like to work with. But they don't have openings for interns. Instead of continuing to look for a similar place that does have an internship program, why not contact the organization and see if they'd like to establish one. Track down the head of the department you'd like to intern in or arrange to talk to the organization's president or personnel director. Let your contact know how beneficial it would be for the company to start hiring interns . . . starting with you! They'll get enthusiastic help with current projects, have replacement hands when employees go on vacation, and have the opportunity to train and recruit excellent potential hires. If you're a student, an advisor in your internship office will probably be glad to help you make your case to the employer and help the company set up a program. The accompanying CD includes guidelines that will help get a program under way.

If you're no longer a student or the organization isn't ready to start a full-fledged internship program, you can suggest an externship or a shadowing program (which would allow you to observe particular employees as they went about their work, during a day or over a several-week period). Taking part in such a program will still give you a good chance to learn about the company and the field.

Do you have some ideas of your own? Being creative may get you where you want to go. So be determined and keep trying. You may just end up with the perfect internship for you.

Chapter 6
Opportunities for Graduates and Career Changers

In the previous chapter, we outlined all the different types of internships and career-related experiences that are available to help you narrow down your interests and goals. Some of those possibilities, though, are open only to students still pursuing their B.A. or B.S. But if you've already graduated from college and are either in graduate school or out in the workforce—or your company downsized or you've taken a break from working to travel or raise a family—and now you're ready to jump back in, don't worry. There are plenty of options open to you to try out different career paths, refresh or expand your skills, and boost your chances of getting hired in a job you'll love.

Internships and related options aren't only for teenagers and early twenty-somethings. While some people may tell you that internships are worthwhile only if you do them before you leave college or before you enter the working world, that's really not the case.

TEACHING WITH A TESL

An important option for anyone who's completed a bachelor's degree is teaching, either abroad or in the United States. To enhance your chances of landing a teaching position, to see if education is a field to pursue, it's a great idea to earn an additional certificate, either a Teaching English as a Second Language (TESL) or a Teaching English as a Foreign Language (TEFL) certificate. Holders of one of these certificates generally have additional, and better paid, possibilities—especially in other parts of the world.

To find out more about taking the TESL or TEFL certification course (you can often take it for credit), check one of these Web sites:

- www.humnet.ucla.edu.humnet/al/frames/mahome.htm
- www.unex.ucla.edu
- www.americanlanguage.org
- www.telfboard.org

Internships are great vehicles at any stage of your life to explore what's out there and see if it's for you.

Internships can be especially valuable before applying to graduate school and when you're thinking of making a career change. In boom times, many graduates opt for skipping additional education in favor of taking a high-paying job, which means that if you choose to apply to grad school there won't be as much competition. But in a down economy, such as the one we've been experiencing, applications to graduate schools go way up; when people can't find work, they often decide to go back to school to gain new skills and improve their qualifications. If you've been thinking of doing that very thing, doing an internship first might prove to be a better move. That's because, while you learn more about a particular field, the economy may improve, resulting in fewer competing applications when you're ready to send yours in. The added experience will also look great on your résumé, and you'll have the real-world business know-how that grad schools often require. Not only that, but you'll be able to confirm that you're on a career track you want to be on before you invest more time and money in extra years in school. And speaking of money, if you can find a paid internship or fellowship, you'll be able to add to your grad school kitty while you add to your knowledge, confidence, and capabilities.

If you're already going to graduate school but want to sample what a career would be like before you commit to a job, doing a post-college internship will give you that opportunity. And if you're already part of the working world but are feeling burned out or wondering if you took a wrong turn somewhere, doing an internship can also be a great move. The job you've been holding down may have been perfect for you at one point, but people's interests and skills do change over time, and you may be ready for something new to match your later-in-life dreams or goals—or dreams that you once had that were pushed aside to meet obligations.

Alice, for example, took a job right after graduation with one of the Big Five financial firms. Her parents had always encouraged her to find a good, stable career that would bring her the income they had never had. But after a few years, Alice owned up to the fact that she was miserable. Yes, she was earning a good living, but the work didn't challenge her, and she never had a feeling of excitement or satisfaction.

What did make her extremely happy, though, was mentoring young girls through a volunteer group she belonged to. After talking to a counselor there, she decided to take the plunge. She quit her job and signed up for a one-year volunteer stint with World Teach, a nonprofit organization affiliated with Harvard University's Center for International Development. All she needed was her bachelor's degree and the desire to explore some options. After a year working with children in Ecuador, Alice realized that teaching was her passion, and returned to the states to start studying for a teaching credential and a career in education.

Doing an internship, or taking advantage of one of the other options available to those out of school, can also be a great way to return after a time away from the job market. If you haven't been working for a while, you may have decided that you really don't want to go back to what you did before, that you never felt comfortable doing it, or that it just didn't fulfill your needs. Or volunteer work or other activities you've been involved in may have made you aware of interests you never realized were important to you. But since you don't have any on-the-job experience in those areas and aren't certain of your skills, actually getting a job outside your former field may seem impossible. An internship can help with that—it will let you determine if you really want to go in the new direction and give you the experience and the expertise that future employers will want you to have.

Checking Out Your Choices

So just what are the opportunities for those who are no longer undergraduates? Basically, they are fellowships; studying, volunteering, interning, researching, and teaching in the United States or abroad; research opportunities; and language-school programs (see Chapter 3 for descriptions of all of these options). There are also internships (we're going to use the term generally in this chapter to refer to any of the available options that last from a couple of weeks to two years) that can actually be converted to a full-time job when you complete them. For example, the Presidential Management Internship program (www.pmi.opm.gov), for people with a master's or doctorate from an accredited college or university, appoints selected interns to a two-year position as a GS-9 employee (this is a government services ranking). At the end of the two years, interns can convert their position into a career or a career-conditional job and become eligible for promotion to a GS-12 level; the pay at that level is about $51,000. This and all of the other possibilities are remarkable ways to improve and increase your skills, broaden your outlook, and give you a big advantage in your quest for a great job.

When you start to think about which careers you'd like to look into, try to keep an open mind. Just because you majored in political science in college doesn't mean you have to look for a related opportunity—you can try something completely new. Think about your personality, your style, the environment you're most comfortable in. Assess your character traits and skills with one of the tests described in Chapter 2. Also think about talking with friends, current or former colleagues, professors, other alumni from your college or university, other people in an organization or volunteer group you belong to, career counselors and coaches, and people working in fields you're considering. You can also check career-oriented Web sites like www.vault.com both for coaching services for those reentering the workforce and for write-ups on hundreds of employers. Finally, you should think hard about your dreams: If you could have any job in the world, what would it be?

Also consider the possibility that you started out on the right track, but somewhere along the way took the wrong fork. For example, you might feel burned out working for a large government agency, but the problem might be the size of the office, not the job; you might be much happier doing similar work in a small public policy office. That kind of knowledge can help you figure out which type of internship or fellowship to apply for to see if the new position is really what you're looking for.

If your circumstances allow it—say, you've retired from one career or you don't have family responsibilities—think about making a really big leap and trying on a new career or learning new skills abroad. It doesn't have to be expensive; for example, the Peace Corps, in which you could improve your language skills for a job in foreign affairs by sharing your business expertise with third-world entrepreneurs, will pay your living expenses and give you a check for $6,000 when you finish your twenty-seven-month commitment. And as far as money in general goes, most fellowships are paid positions, and scholarships and other sources of funding are available to work and study both at home and abroad (see the appendix for possibilities). If you give yourself the freedom to think outside the box and the chance to do something you might not have been able to do earlier in your life, there is probably a way to make it happen.

But just like an undergraduate applying for an internship, you need to put in the time to consider the possibilities, research all the available opportunities, and put your best foot forward in the application and interview process (see Chapter 4 for help finding and narrowing down internship and fellowship choices and Chapter 8 for great tips on the best ways to present yourself). And if you decide to go abroad, you need to be aware of cultural differences and be sensitive to international issues. Your alumni association, local library, or local adult education school may have information or workshops on traveling abroad, and your college career center may also offer workshops.

If it's been a while since you applied for any kind of work-related position, you're probably going to need to update your résumé. Here again your alumni association or college career center may be able to help, and we provide a number of sample résumés on the CD that can also be of help. If you're not confident about your interviewing skills or they're a bit rusty, check Chapter 8 for tips. You can also see if your alumni organization will set up a mock interview for you with an alum in an area you're thinking of looking into. Or find a friend or former colleague who's still in the working world who'd be willing to refresh you on what is currently required. Things may have changed—from how to submit your résumé to how to dress—since you last applied for a position!

A Cross-Section of Possible Programs

To give you an idea of the kinds of post-college opportunities available, read about the following programs to see if one catches your fancy. Web sites for tracking down additional possibilities are also included in the accompanying CD. And if you learn about a great-sounding internship that's focused on undergrads, check it out anyway; there's always the chance that the company or agency will make an exception for someone pursuing a dream.

Teach for America

The Teach for America program provides opportunities for college graduates from all academic majors. Each year approximately two thousand men and women are selected for two-year positions teaching children in urban and rural public schools in eighteen locations around the country, from New York City to the Mississippi Delta to New Mexico. Participants are trained at summer institutes and then placed as full-time paid teachers. A support network helps participants ensure that underrepresented children have an equal chance at a successful life (www.teachforamerica.org).

Rotary Ambassadorial Scholarships

To further international understanding and positive relationships among countries, the Rotary Club offers several scholarships that enable recipients to study abroad. In addition to their studies, recipients also act as goodwill ambassadors, speaking to host-country organizations about life in the United States. When their year of study is over, scholars share their experiences with Rotary groups and other organizations back home. Scholarships are available for undergraduates, graduates, and professionals pursuing vocational studies (www.rotary.org/foundation/educational/amb_scho).

The Herbert Scoville Jr. Peace Fellowship Program

The fellowships available through the Herbert Scoville Jr. Peace Fellowship Program (based in Washington, D.C.) are open to college graduates with a strong interest in peace and security issues, particularly those with previous experience in public-interest advocacy. Positions last for six to nine months, and may be in one of twenty-three organizations affiliated with the program. Fellowship recipients get involved with such things as research, writing, and other activities that support the organization they're working with (www.clw.org/pub/clw/scoville).

The CORO Fellows Program

Each year sixty-four individuals are chosen for the highly selective CORO Fellows Program. Applicants may have just about any background, range of interests, and academic or work experience, but should be firmly committed to excellence in public affairs. Fellows work in nine-month-long full-time positions in either New York, Pittsburgh, Los Angeles, St. Louis, or San Francisco. They handle field assignments, site visits, interviews, and special projects. The CORO program is focused on post-graduate leadership training (www.coro.org).

The Minority Management Development Program

The year-long Minority Management Development Program provides minority graduates interested in health care with practical experience in managed care. Fellows work closely with a preceptor who mentors them, and they learn through both academic and experiential situations (www.ahip.org/content/default.aspx?bc-40195).

Overseas Press Club Foundation Scholarships

Graduates and undergraduates who are interested in becoming foreign correspondents are encouraged to apply for Overseas Press Club scholarships. The focus of the program is to "improve the media's understanding of international issues and raise the quality of newsgathering efforts in covering the world" (www.opcofamerica.org).

Pacific Legal Foundation Fellowships

The College of Public Interest Law offers one- and two-year fellowships for studying and researching legal and public-policy issues. The fellowships are open to recent graduates and attorneys who recently became members of the bar (www.pacificlegal.org).

Museum Education Graduate Fellowship

The Art Institute of Chicago offers this fellowship to graduates interested in a museum education career. Designed to promote professional growth, the fellowship is open to current graduate students or those who recently completed a graduate program with a concentration in art (www.artic.edu).

The American Prospect Fellowship

Several fellowships are available through the liberal bi-monthly *American Prospect* magazine, which reports on politics, culture, economics, and policy. Recipients participate in seminars with leading journalists and work closely with *American Prospect* editors to develop their own style and focus. During the year-long fellowship, fellows produce articles for both *American Prospect* and other national magazines (www.prospect.org).

New York Urban Fellows Program

This New York City–based program introduces college graduates to local government and public-sector service. The nine-month program combines full-time employment with a seminar series that lets participants explore the workings of big-city government as well as issues facing the Big Apple. Fellows work in virtually every area of governing: budget planning, agency operations, low-income housing, affordable health care, education, and economic development (www. nyc.gov/html/dcas/html/urbanfellows.html).

AmeriCorps

AmeriCorps is involved in a multitude of community-based projects. It lets volunteers of all ages learn new skills and find their passion while helping others across the country. After taking on a challenge such as tutoring kids, building houses, restoring coastlines, or helping victims of domestic violence, participants are able to apply for several thousand dollars in education awards for use at a qualified institute of higher learning (www.americorps.org).

The AT&T Labs Fellowship Program

The AT&T fellowships offer support to women and minority students beginning Ph.D. programs with a focus in a scientific field of importance to the company. Fellowships are renewable for up to six years if recipients continue progressing in their Ph.D. program. Fellowships are available in communications, computer science, electrical engineering, human computer interaction, industrial engineering, information science, math, operations research, and statistics (www.research.att.com/academic).

The Jerome Levy Economics Institute Forecasting Fellowship

A B.A. in economics or a related field is needed to apply for a Forecasting Fellowship at the Jerome Levy Economics Institute. Fellows work with the director of forecasting to analyze sectors of the economy and contribute to the development of a macroeconomic forecast (www.levy.org).

National Security Education Program

Through the National Security Education Program, scholarships are available to U.S. citizens who want to study abroad in areas considered critical to national security; this excludes western Europe, Canada, Australia, and New Zealand. Applicants must be interested in undertaking serious study in a foreign country as a complement to either their academic or their career goals (www.iie.org/template.cfm?&template-/programs/nsep/default.htm).

Hostelling International Travel Grant

A $500 Hostelling International grant is awarded to an applicant between the ages of seventeen and twenty-six who designs a project that will inspire others to stay in hostels while traveling. The winner must submit his or her idea to the grant committee after the completion of travel (www.lahostels.org//programs.htm#tg).

Global Volunteers

Through the Global Volunteers, you can live and work with people in other parts of the world to improve language skills, share your expertise, and learn about a new culture. Volunteers support over a hundred host communities on six continents throughout the year. The one-, two- and three-week-long projects center on child care, tutoring, teaching English, environmental work, construction, health care, and more. No special skills are required (www.globalvolunteers.org).

The U.S. Department of Energy's Graduate Fellowship Programs

Fellowships available through the Department of Energy let graduates learn about energy development, environmental management, and energy-personnel safety. Former holders of these fellowships are now leaders in energy research and development (www.atmos.anl.gov/gcep).

Fulbright Grants and Teaching Assistantships

The Fulbright Program, known for its work promoting international exchange and learning, provides grants and assistantships in a number of fields, including travel, business, and teaching. Many opportunities exist for recent graduates, post-graduate candidates, and professionals and artists who want to add to their knowledge and skills by studying, teaching, or doing research abroad (www.iie.org/fulbright).

The Japan Exchange and Teaching Program (JET)

The JET program gives those with a strong interest in Japanese culture a chance to take part in foreign language education in various sites throughout Japan. Participants, who are paid, can serve in local government organizations as well as teach English in public and private junior and senior high schools. Applicants need to hold a B.A. in any subject, have excellent English language skills, and be forty years old or younger (www.mofa.go.jp/jet).

The Peace Corps

Like AmeriCorps, the Peace Corps is a great place to expand your world, consider taking a new direction in life, build skills, and find clarity as well as adventure, all while contributing to making the world a better place. As a Peace Corps volunteer, you might counsel teens, teach high-school chemistry, promote AIDS awareness, help develop a small business, set up a computer-learning center, or assist with any number of educational and community-oriented activities in just about any part of the world. Anyone eighteen or older is eligible to volunteer (the oldest Peace Corps volunteer so far was eighty-three), and the organization partners with universities across the United States to offer academic credit and financial incentives to undergrads and grads during or after their twenty-seven-month service. The Peace Corps also offers a fellows program that provides scholarships or reduced tuition to volunteers after they complete their service (www.peacecorps.gov).

The INNexperience

Burned-out techies and other members of the business world might want to try something completely different by taking classes in inn-keeping and then "inn-sitting" to see if they might like the career. This program, with locations across the country, provides five-day sessions to anyone interested in learning how to run a bed and breakfast (B&B) or inn. The training, including tips on finding short-term inn-sitting positions while the owners are away or need extra help, gives participants the chance to see if inn-keeping might be a good second career or retirement job or if they might want to be full-time B&B owners themselves (www.innsitter.bigstep.com).

Chapter 7
What Employers Want

Contrary to what a few misinformed people may have told you—that employers hire interns only for an inexpensive or, better yet, free, source of labor; that they give interns only busy work or grunt work rather than real responsibility; or that they don't really care about interns or their interests and goals—most employers take their internship programs, as well as their interns, quite seriously. If they're not genuinely looking for immediate, results-oriented help and the opportunity to train or evaluate potential employees and help new people up the ladder, they won't want to take the time and energy needed to set up and administer an internship program.

So the first thing many employers want you to know is that they do want great interns in their office, and they do want you to succeed. Yes, they may be able to take you on for less money than they would pay a full-time employee, which will of course help their bottom line. But the longer-term benefits to their organization generally are more important: everything from having a great source of future hires who are likely to stay with the company for a while to learning what's going on in the college and young-adult market to saving money and time searching for new hires to giving junior-level managers the chance to gain supervisory experience. By hiring interns, employers can try candidates out for prospective positions in the company without making major commitments, and they may also profit from the good PR that having an internship program can generate. Indirectly, they may benefit from your talking up the company and either encouraging other interns to apply there or urging friends or relatives who are actively looking for work to consider their organization.

In other words, most employers are going to think of you as an asset, not just a set of hands that they have to keep busy.

But—and weren't you sure there was going to be a *but*!—you need to be up to the challenge. And prospective employers are going to be checking you out to be as certain as they can be that you *are* up to the challenge.

What are they looking for? Here are some important things that employers and supervisors have singled out, which we encourage you to keep in mind as you go through the application and interning process.

Have Those Basic Skills

When you apply for an internship, many employers will want you to have certain specific skills. For example, an internship with a TV news program might require that you have good research skills to help develop story ideas. An internship at an archaeological center might ask you to demonstrate strong teaching skills, so that you can help educate schoolchildren or other visitors to the center. Some openings will require that you have particular technical training that's needed on the job; for example, you might need HTML experience to work with a Web designer. Each internship description will detail the skills you need to have.

In addition to those specifics, however, most employers are also looking for basic interpersonal and communication skills; they want you to be able to get along with and work with others and to be able to express yourself both orally and in writing. So when you list your qualifications on an application or in an interview, it's a good idea to include experiences you've had working on a team, making oral presentations, and preparing reports or other forms of written communication. Presenting yourself well in an interview and being enthusiastic yet professional on the job will also help to keep you in good stead (see later in this chapter and in Chapter 8 for tips).

Another skill that more and more employers are seeing as basic is being proficient at the computer. Unless the internship you want is a technical one, this doesn't mean you have to run out and start learning programming languages. But it does mean that you should probably be able to do word processing and be familiar with standard software (such as *Word*) and at least have an inkling of how to navigate the information superhighway. If you're a complete technophobe, this may be a good time to take a beginning class at your college or at a local community college or adult-education center.

Have a Good Attitude

During the course of writing this book, we found that many employers believe one of the most important qualifications an intern can bring to the job is the right attitude. This means being enthusiastic, being positive, and being ready to contribute and take on responsibilities. It does *not* mean acting superior, being a know-it-all, being lazy, or doing anything but your best. While you may not need a lot of experience to win an internship, you do need to demonstrate that you want it and will work hard at it—and that you'll be someone the rest of the office staff will be happy to be around. Having a great attitude can give you the edge if your qualifications and those of the other candidates are pretty much the same. It can also help you get the most out of the entire internship experience.

For example, Karen, a Cornell junior, spent most of her internship at a women's health network doing research and writing letters. Toward the end of the internship, the work started to seem awfully repetitive. But instead of getting bored or disinterested, Karen asked if she could also help organize an upcoming march. Not only were her employers happy to have her help but they were impressed by her enthusiasm and her problem-solving attitude. And Karen, of course, increased her knowledge by taking on another aspect of the job.

Have More Than a Great GPA

If you're attending or have graduated from an accredited college, it certainly won't hurt if your transcript shows top grades. But it's important to remember that, while employers (and we!) applaud your academic achievement, you're probably not going to be the only internship candidate with a strong GPA. Most employers are looking for someone who does well in the classroom, but they're also looking for someone who is well rounded and involved outside the classroom walls.

When you apply for an internship or take part in an interview, be sure to mention relevant real-world experiences that you've had. This can include campus activities you've participated in, groups you belong to, community service work you've done, other internships you've completed, political or activist campaigns you've supported, travel abroad, the fact that you speak and use a second language—anything that shows you're engaged and interested in the wider world.

Not having nonacademic interests and experience can definitely hurt you. Sam, an economics major, applied for eight internship opportunities but received only one offer to interview. Though his grades were pretty solid, he hadn't taken part in any extra-curricular activities, and he learned later that more than two-thirds of his competition had been involved in groups like the campus economics club. Not only did he miss out on all the opportunities these types of clubs provide, such as networking and mock interviews, but he also deprived himself of a chance to learn and grow in the real world, which limited him in the eyes of potential employers.

If you're thinking of applying for an internship during the next year and you haven't been involved in a lot of non-school-related activities, this would be a good time to explore some possibilities. Just be sure your choices won't only be statistics to list on your application, but experiences you'll enjoy and find meaningful.

Remember It's a Short-Term Learning Experience, Not a Long-Term Job

While it may seem obvious that an internship has a fixed end point, some interns forget they've been taken on for the short term and have set responsibilities. They wonder why they're not offered the same benefits and opportunities as full-time employees. An internship is a chance for you to get know an organization and for the organization's staff to get to know you, but it's important to remember that you're not being hired and you won't be given full benefits. Once you've completed your internship, you *may* receive an offer of employment, but that doesn't always happen. In fact, some organizations even require that you be a continuing student with at least one quarter of school to complete before they'll offer you an internship. These offices, including many government agencies and media companies, want to make sure that interns understand the opening is for just the specified period and that they're expected to return to school. Often a potential employer will ask someone in your career center or internship office to verify that you're a continuing student, and some agencies, including the Department of Justice, will require that you sign a form agreeing that you won't be compensated, won't accrue vacation, and won't receive other typical benefits that full-time employees are entitled to.

Don't Overdo It

Yes, employers do want you to be enthusiastic and excited about being their intern. But both in the interview and on the job, they don't want you to be obnoxious! Wyatt, the editor of a sports magazine, says that candidates who try too hard or are overly anxious to please are a real turnoff and that a friendly, positive manner is what you want to aim for. Being too chummy or ingratiating or way too overeager can put up barriers to a good experience; it's likely that people will start avoiding you instead of wanting to encourage you. Do be upbeat and confident in an interview (see Chapter 8 for more interview tips) and do search out ways to help if you complete your assignments early. Be sure to support your supervisor and anyone else who needs a hand, but don't be annoying, it will definitely work against you.

Expect to Do Some Grunt Work

Although the main tasks you're given as an intern should be meaty and involve real skills, some of the time it's likely that you'll be handling less than exciting jobs. This work isn't given to you to take advantage of you or your position, but to have you help out with time-consuming work that everyone has to deal with. For example, Lexy, a Southwest Airlines supervisor, said that interns are asked to pitch in with menial jobs because everyone else in the office does them too—washing coffee mugs, sending faxes, making copies, filing paperwork, shelving supplies, answering the phones. So keep in mind that most internships will require some administrative or clerical work. To find out how much, read position descriptions carefully. If you don't see a breakdown there, be sure to ask during the interview. You shouldn't spend your entire internship making address changes in customer files or picking up the boss's latte—and if you do, you should bring this to your supervisor's attention and, if nothing changes, quit rather than waste more time. But the reality is that every duty won't be inspiring.

Do Your Homework

When you apply for an internship, employers want you to be sure that you have a good sense of their organization—they want you to know about their products and services, their mission, their culture, their history. Armed with that information, you'll be certain *before* the interview that they're actually involved in work you're interested in doing, so no one's time is wasted. You may also get an inkling of how you might fit into their organization. Researching the company will also reflect your enthusiasm for working there, a big plus for making a good impression in the interview and helping you answer questions an interviewer will likely ask.

Nick, the president of a Spanish-language public-interest radio station, won't even talk to a potential intern before he or she studies the company's Web site. That's because Nick looks for interns who are not only interested in mass communication but want to change the world, something the station is working to do. By reading up on the company, potential interns see that not only does the station broadcast news and information, but it gets involved in political activities, festivals, lobbying members of Congress, providing a help line for listeners, supporting women's rights and environmental causes—all kinds of activities that can affect social change. While interns need to be interested in learning about running a national broadcasting operation, they also need to have an interest in causes the station supports. When applying for any position, doing some research can help you ensure a good fit.

Brushing up on the organizations you're interested in can benefit you in another way: It can help your eventual employer figure out departments in the company that might suit you best. For example, if you're interested in learning about being a radio station studio engineer, most likely you'd spend most of your time working with an engineer. But if you learn that, like Nick's station, the radio station you're interested in helps community members start non-profits for social causes, your employer might be able to arrange for you to get a wider experience. For instance, you might be able to spend time in administration, finance, the department in which grant proposals are written—all the areas you would need to learn about to start and run a non-profit.

Act Professionally

OK, this isn't a full-time, long-term job, right? You're an intern, not an employee. But that doesn't mean you can act any less businesslike than everyone else in the organization; your employer will expect you to dress and behave the same, no matter how young or old you are. That means if you're used to hanging out in jeans and T-shirts, you'll need to show up in more appropriate business attire (unless you intern with a creative organization that tells you that jeans and Ts *are* office attire). If you're often late for class or appointments, you'll need to change your ways; it's important to be at your desk at the start of the day and stay until the close of business. And if you're used to doing your own thing, remember that, while creativity and innovation are important and usually welcome, if you're asked to follow specific directions it's not a time to forge ahead with your own plan.

It's also important to keep in mind that you need to act like the mature and sensible person you are. If you're having issues at home, you need to leave them there; don't mope around the office or take up other people's time asking for sympathy or advice (you, of course, want to be friendly and open, but being overly emotional is not proper business behavior). One supervisor at a government agency recounted the time an intern went into a high-level meeting, after asking for weeks to be allowed to attend, and burst into tears because she was going through a hard time with her boyfriend. The meeting was disrupted, and the intern remained at her desk for the duration of her internship.

TEN TOP WAYS TO SHINE

- Be a great communicator.

- Be open to learning and doing things in new ways.

- Dress and act in a businesslike manner.

- Be positive and upbeat.

- Pitch in and contribute wherever you can.

- Ask questions to learn more.

- Take on all you can, but not more than you can handle.

- Thank everyone who helps you.

- Take advantage of each opportunity.

- Do your best in everything you do.

Another important part of acting responsibly is being honest. If you don't understand an assignment, speak up and say so. It's much better to ask for clarification than to jump into a project and do it wrong. If you don't think you can handle a job, ask for help or more information. And if you do screw something up, just admit it. Most supervisors understand that you're new to either the working world or the specific job, and they don't expect perfection. They do want you to try your best, but they're also there to help you succeed, and they know that everyone makes a mistake now and then.

Finally, employers want to remind you that you're interning on company time. That means you shouldn't take an extra half hour at lunch to do your grocery shopping or spend hours on the phone making arrangements for your wedding or calling all your friends. The main way you're going to learn from your experience and give yourself the internship advantage is to put in the time and do the best job you can.

Expect to Be Checked Out

Many employers look at internships as a great way to recruit future employees, so they're going to be assessing your work and watching how you handle yourself. This will probably start right at the interview. If you say you can do something on your résumé, you'll be expected to be able to do it. If you're asked for references, more than likely those people will be called. If you're scheduled to come in for an interview at 3:30, the interviewer will note if you drift in excuse-free at 3:45. And if you're dressed sloppily or forget to bring requested paperwork, it will be seen as a sign that you're not taking the internship, or your future, seriously.

On the job, the same thing will hold true. While we hope no one will be continually looking over your shoulder, a supervisor will probably be assigned to you not only to orient and train you but to administer your workload and see how you're progressing. Some internships have scheduled weekly or monthly review meetings in which you can expect to be asked about the projects you've been working on; others have a more informal process, with periodic check-ins. If you're doing an internship for credit, you will probably also be monitored by the professor sponsoring your internship or by someone in his or her office. Many internships also conclude with an evaluation meeting with the employer, which could cover anything from how you handle yourself under deadlines to your ability to work as part of a team to skills that need improvement to strengths you brought to the job.

In other words, be prepared to have your skills and work ethic evaluated before, during, and at the end of your internship.

Don't Take on More Than You Can Handle

Employers want you to know that you're not the only one hoping your internship will be fulfilling; they also want you to succeed and be satisfied. A lot of your success will have to do with your attitude and applying yourself. But some of it will also depend on how much energy you have. That means fitting your internship into your schedule and your life and not letting it overwhelm you. If you're going to be taking classes or working part-time, or be involved in a huge number of outside activities, try to keep your internship hours to no more than ten or twelve (or fewer) a week. If you accept a full-time internship and you know you may be asked to work on weekends or at odd times or a good amount of overtime, try to keep your other projects to a minimum during the course of the job. Coming to work with a good night's sleep will help you not only enjoy the experience and do your best but get out of it what you're looking for—and satisfy your employer's goals as well. And that, of course, can also help you in the long run, with a great letter of recommendation or, better yet, a fantastic job offer. Finally, if you do well and your employer is happy, he or she will be encouraged to keep the internship program going, which will benefit many other interns who follow.

A Successful Experience—for Intern *and* Employer

With his last year of college fast approaching, Charlie Roberts had no idea of what he wanted to do after graduation. He had just returned from a semester studying abroad and realized he would need to make some decisions in the near future. Three things had crossed his mind whenever he had thought about his career previously: investment banking, accounting work, and consulting. Now that it was time to think more seriously, he realized that, from what he knew, investment banking would be a more intense environment than he'd be happy in and consulting would be a hard way to start out, although it might be something he could do when he had more experience. As an accounting minor, he'd had a pretty good look into the field and thought it might be the way to go.

But though he had taken several accounting classes, Charlie had no hands-on knowledge. "I had pretty solid grades," Charlie says. "But I was a little behind in the experience column. There's a major difference between what you learn from a textbook and what you actually do on the job." To get the experience he needed, both for the skills he would develop and for a strong addition to his résumé, he decided to test the waters by doing an accounting internship the following summer.

Research time in his college's internship office produced several possibilities with the Big Four accounting firms. Charlie focused on these because he knew from his classes that they were international companies with excellent reputations and that he would get great exposure in any one of them. He applied quickly—it was January, and several of the firms had January 31 application deadlines for their summer openings—and he received several interview offers. After one round of interviews, he was asked back for a second interview at KPMG's Los Angeles office.

The second interview was four hours long, much longer than Charlie had anticipated. But KPMG, like a number of other companies, interviews interns with the intention of having them become full-time employees. "The company spends a lot of time and money on prospective interns," Charlie relates. "They want the interns they choose to turn into full-time hires, so the interview process is pretty serious and involved. They want to take on interns who they think will be a good match with the company."

In addition to the two interviews, there were several social events to attend, from lunches and dinners to a sports event, with various partners and managers. "I enjoyed all the meals and entertainment," Charlie reports, "but it was draining, too, because I had to be on my most professional behavior."

But it all paid off. Charlie was offered the internship.

When he started as an intern, Charlie was placed in the audit department. But for the first week of the program, none of the interns worked in the office. (KPMG takes on nearly eight hundred interns each year in their offices across the country.) All of the interns were sent to Palm Springs, where they had orientation sessions and underwent specific training. For several hours a day, they attended classes in which they learned more about the company, their own responsibilities, how to network, the shoulds and shouldn'ts of working with clients, interviewing techniques, and much more. For the last three days, all the interns from the Los Angeles office trained together, so they were able to get to know each other before settling into the office routine.

That routine actually wasn't routine at all. After a week of in-office training, Charlie worked directly with clients, spending a week or two with one company and then moving on to another. "When you work in auditing," Charlie explains, "you're verifying that a publicly traded company's financial statements are accurate, that their accounting is done properly, and that there's no fraud. My office was working with close to forty companies at the same time, so I got involved with firms in a variety of industries. Plus we went to the clients' sites, they didn't come to our office. The idea is to give interns experience with many different businesses so they can see which type of companies they might want to work with if they stay, like banking and financial firms or entertainment organizations."

Because the company hires interns who they hope will eventually sign on, they treat the interns as first-year, entry-level employees. Charlie says he did a small amount of copying, faxing, and phone answering, but most of his responsibilities were significant. "I was part of a team, of from one to ten other people, who went to clients' sites and interacted with the staff there. I checked numbers, wrote memos, and basically did what the full-time employees did."

He also received the kind of perks full-time employees receive: a laptop; a business credit card; business cards; and several paid outings, including a full day at Disneyland and one to Catalina Island. He also received an hourly wage that was almost comparable to what an entry-level employee made.

But Charlie worked hard at his job, learning about auditing practices and improving his skills. "I had a good understanding of most of the basic computer programs before I started working there," he says. "Which was important, because about half the work I did involved the computer. But I learned about a lot of features I'd never used before that really helped me in my work."

To keep Charlie involved with a steady flow of projects, he was assigned a supervisor who accompanied him to clients' offices. He also had a "buddy," a full-time employee who had been at the company for a year or so who he could go to with questions he might not want to ask his supervisor. When he started at the company, Charlie and his buddy were given $200 to spend on dinners or ball games or other getting-acquainted events.

A third person Charlie was assigned to was a performance manager. This was a manager who was fairly high up in the company and who reviewed how Charlie was doing after his ten weeks on the job. As part of the review process, Charlie filled out a form evaluating how he thought he was doing and what he needed to work on. Then his supervisor added his comments, and both reviews were sent to the performance manager.

In his exit interview, at the end of the ten-week internship, the manager and Charlie discussed how everything had gone—what Charlie had liked and not liked, what was most memorable, what he had learned. The interview took about a half hour, but according to Charlie, "It wasn't too intense." And the best part was that he was offered a full-time job.

It was just what Charlie was hoping for. But before accepting—he was given two months to say yes or no—he decided to make absolutely sure of his commitment to the field and to earn some additional money by doing another internship with the company during his final quarter at school. At present, he's pretty sure he'll accept the position, but spending another ten weeks working there will make him feel certain.

What advice does he have for future interns? "When you're being recruited, as well as when you're interning, you want to make a good impression but without going nuts. Remember to have fun too. And do as much networking as you can. You'll find out what other people do, which will help you understand the business better. And if you end up working there full time, you'll already know a lot of the staff, which can benefit you on the job. Several people I met have told me that if I decide to sign on with KPMG, they want to put me on their team."

Charlie also has some advice for employers. "The first week of orientation really was helpful. I learned a lot about how business is conducted, and I also got to know a bunch of people I later worked with. So I felt pretty comfortable and could get right to work as soon as we were back in the office. It was also great to have a 'buddy' who could answer all my questions. My internship definitely helped me come closer to a decision about whether accounting is right for me. And all the support I got made it a great experience."

Chapter 8
Ace the Application Process

Once you've narrowed down your choices to the internships that seem like your top opportunities and you've got a good handle on what employers will be looking for, it's time to take the next step: applying for the positions. But applying for an internship doesn't just mean filling out a form and sending it in. There are three distinct parts of the process

- Completing the application, which in addition to filling out a form may include creating a résumé—either a traditional résumé or the new alternative, the Q letter—writing a cover letter or a statement of interest; and providing additional materials such as writing samples, letters of recommendation, published articles or a portfolio, or a copy of your transcript

- Being interviewed

- Following up

Because the first two parts can take some time and because deadlines can be short—many summer openings have an application deadline of the previous fall—it's a good idea to get going as soon as you've made your internship picks.

Acing the Application

The most important point to remember about an application is that it's *the* thing that will get you an interview, which is what you're after if you're applying for a local position. An interview lets you put a person behind your name and showcase your fabulous skills and enthusiasm. If an interview isn't a possibility (if you're applying for an opening in another part of the country or abroad) and you won't be able to get there for a face-to-face meeting, your application is *the* thing that will win you the job.

Feeling a little pressure? Don't let it get you down. While the intern selection process can be competitive and different employers will request different types of information from you, the following tips can help you pull together an application package that makes you and your talents shine.

The Form

Few employers still ask interns to complete an application form; most want to see a résumé and/or other application materials. For example, if you applied for an internship at the Museum of Modern Art in New York City, there would be no form to fill out; instead, you'd be ask to submit your contact information; a résumé that includes both your education and employment history; two letters of recommendation; an official transcript; a list of art history or related courses you've taken; reference to any foreign languages you know; and a five-hundred-word essay describing your career goals, interest in museum work, and the reasons you're applying.

However, some companies still do require that you fill out their form. If that's the case for one of your choices, either ask the organization to mail it to you or see if you can download it from its Web site (if all the company wants is an application, you may be able to complete and send it in online). Then be sure to read and answer the questions carefully; it's a good idea to read the whole application first before you start filling in any boxes. Once you've completed the form, ask someone with an eye for it to make sure you didn't leave anything out or make any typos. Also be sure to check for and enclose all additional information that's asked for, such as a letter of recommendation or a statement of interest.

The Cover Letter

If you're going to be sending in more than just an application form, you'll need to write a cover letter to accompany your materials. What exactly is a cover letter? It's really like a brief résumé in that it points out your skills and experience. But the true purpose of a cover letter is to get the person who receives it to take the time to read your complete application. The cover letter is actually a marketing tool; it should catch the reader's interest and persuade him or her to dig in more deeply.

To make your cover letter succeed, you need to:

- Target your message

- Spotlight your accomplishments

- Focus on what you have to offer

Begin your letter by typing in your name, address, and contact information. Also include the date. Then, in a separate section, type the name, title, company, and address of the person listed in the internship description. If no name is given, call the organization or check online to see if you can find the name of the person who's likely to make the employment decision. Readers appreciate being addressed as Mr. or Ms. MyRealName rather than "To whom it may concern" (just be sure to spell the name correctly!); having a name to write to will also make it more likely that your letter will actually reach someone in charge rather than make the rounds of the entire organization. It will also give you someone to follow up with later. If you search and search but can't come up with the appropriate person, you can use "To whom it may concern" or just start your letter with "Good morning."

Begin the body of the letter by stating the internship or other option you're applying for and how you heard of it. Then, in just a sentence or two, say why the opportunity interests you and a little bit about who you are. For example:

> I'll be graduating in June with a degree in psychology from American University. I believe my classroom training and my related work experience make me a great candidate for your internship and that the experience will help me provide excellent service to future clients.

Then really sell yourself—this is no time to be shy. Tell the reader exactly why you're qualified for the internship. Briefly describe (in one or two paragraphs) two or three major accomplishments that highlight your creativity, follow-through, communication skills, and problem-solving ability. Be sure to connect the needs of the position to skills you possess:

> Through an internship I did in the human resources department of Interprint, I gained a real understanding of what it takes to work in this field. This knowledge, combined with my computer proficiency, my interpersonal skills, and my organizational skills, allows me to be creative as well as effective. I also have experience with a number of activities important to the human relations field, including drafting job postings and speaking to large groups.

Now, take action—re-emphasize your interest in the opening, ask for an interview, and thank the person you're writing to:

I believe I would be an asset to the California Medical Group and appreciate your taking the time to consider my application. Please contact me at your earliest convenience so we can arrange a meeting in which I can provide you with additional information. You can reach me at (555) 555-5555 or 1234@MyEmail.com.

When you have your letter drafted, read it again and polish any less-than-smooth spots. Check your grammar and spelling (no, "spellcheck" isn't enough) and look for typos; an error-filled letter shows a lack of important skills and may also make the reader think that you're not really interested in the position.

Once you're happy with your letter, show it to a counselor, professor, or colleague and make any needed changes. Then add a "Sincerely yours" and leave a space for your signature; under your signature type your name. Print out a clean copy and sign your letter.

Here are two examples of cover letters.

SAMPLE 1: COVER LETTER

Will N. Tern
5050 Experience Street   intern@mailaccount.com
Sherman Oaks, CA 91043   888-867-5309

August 23, 2005

Mr. John Manager
Internship Coordinator
Big Four Accounting
1234 Financial Street
Los Angeles, CA 90909

Dear Mr. Manager,

I am very interested in participating in the 2006 Big Four Summer Analyst Internship Program. I have spoken about your position in depth to Jill Anderson, a former intern in your office, and I have no doubt that it is an opportunity for me to polish the skills necessary for a successful career in accounting.

A variety of experiences have prepared me to excel in this position.

Internship Requirements	My Qualifications
• Analytical skills	• Experience analyzing marketing strategies, case studies, and productivity reports
• Computer skills	• Advanced knowledge of *Excel, Word, Access, Outlook,* and *Explorer*
• Teamwork ability	• Participation in numerous group activities in both leadership and contributor roles
• Intermediate-level accounting course work	• Accounting minor, completed with 3.8 GPA

By working at several jobs and being part of a number of organizations, I have learned that skills and abilities alone are often not enough. In addition to my skills, I bring a strong work ethic and passion to whatever I choose to do. I feel that my enjoyment of all I get involved in is contagious and often helps others rise to a higher level in their own work.

I look forward to hearing from you so that we can schedule an interview in which we can fully discuss this position. I can be reached at 888-867-5309 or intern@mailaccount.com.

Sincerely,

Will N. Tern

SAMPLE 2: COVER LETTER

Will N. Tern
5050 Experience Street   intern@mailaccount.com
Sherman Oaks, CA 91043   888-867-5309

August 23, 2005

Ms. Elizabeth Supervisor
Internship Coordinator
Denkgroep Foundation
1234 Policy Way
Washington, D.C. 00000

Dear Ms. Supervisor,

I am very interested in interning in your Policy Research Position in the U.S. Studies division during summer 2006. I have often referenced publications from your foundation in my own research, and I am fascinated by the work in which the Denkgroep Foundation is involved. My course work and experiences with state politics will enable me to shine as an intern with your organization.

Before I enrolled as a freshman in a U.S. government seminar at the University of California at Los Angeles, I was unfamiliar with the study of political science. That class opened my eyes to what would soon become my major and motivated me to volunteer on an election campaign for a firsthand look at California state politics. I learned from the experience that voter apathy is a major problem among my age group. This led me to actively promote voter registration on campus and perform in-depth research on the subject. Through these experiences, I have developed excellent research and communication skills; and because of my dedication and hard work, I have been awarded many opportunities to serve as a leader.

I believe that I will be a valuable asset to your organization next summer. I will contact you next week to discuss this opportunity further. In the meantime, you can contact me at 888-867-5309 or intern@mailaccount.com if you need any further information or wish to speak to me sooner.

Sincerely,

Will N. Tern

The Q Letter

A shorter alternative to the cover letter is what's being called the *Q letter,* which stands for "qualifications letter." This form of cover letter is just coming into use, but both career coaches and internship counselors think it may someday replace the traditional cover letter and maybe even the résumé. That's because it's easy to read, to the point, and saves readers time and energy going through stacks of applications.

The Q letter quickly shows how your qualifications fit the position you're applying for. After a brief introduction—something like "In application for your internship position, I am submitting my qualifications"—you list the internship requirements on the left side and your skills and experiences on the right side (describe them briefly, but don't just say yes or no). For example:

Internship Requirements	My Qualifications
Computer skills	Knowledge of *Word, Excel,* and *PowerPoint*
Organizational skills	Organized and promoted two workshops on preventing pollution; work part-time with counselors to help students at campus internship office
Editing skills	Acquired editing skills while interning at *Eye on the Environment* magazine

You close the Q letter with the same kind of thank you and interview request that you do in the standard cover letter, and proof and sign it in the same manner.

While the Q letter requires a bit of extra organization, more and more employers are happy to see it, because they often feel that standard cover letters and résumés don't address their particular opening.

It also gives employers another look at potential interns' organizational and analytical skills.

The Résumé

Your résumé is your big chance to detail all the wonderful experiences and skills you have that make you perfect for the opening. It shouldn't be wordy; one page is best. It should, however, include everything relevant to the particular position you're applying for. If you're applying to several different types of openings, you'll need to refocus each résumé you send out. A generic one won't work—you need to gear what you include and what you say to each opportunity.

Two résumé formats are most often used (though you can modify them to meet your needs): (1) the chronological résumé, in which you list your experience, starting with your most recent, and (2) the functional résumé, in which you concentrate more on your skills, which can be a good choice if you're light on relevant experience and heavier on required skills. Both formats should include your name and contact information, nice and big, right at the top, followed by an objective statement and your educational background.

The objective statement should be brief and strong and slanted to the position you're applying for. If you want to intern with a state legislator's office, for example, you might say:

Objective: To work in a state legislator's office to learn more about the legislative process and to further my goal of serving the public interest

Or if you're looking for an internship with a magazine, you could say:

Objective: To learn about the day-to-day operation of a national publication and further develop my writing and research skills

When you list your educational background, include the name of your college or university, the degree you received or your current year and major, and your GPA if it's over 3.0. If your GPA is not that high, it's not the end of the world; many employers are more interested in your skills than your academic standing, and many believe that if you're a student or alum of an accredited university, you've got what it takes. If you've taken courses or have worked in an area related to your objective, list them in a short paragraph.

If you decide to use a chronological format, now list your work experience, including all previous internships. Put the most recent experience first: title, organization, period of time you worked there, the responsibilities you had, and how you made a difference. Use short, active phrases, such as: "Expanded the program to reach more of Company X's market." Continue in the same way with a chronological list of previous work experiences. But don't go back too far. Potential employers want to know what you've done lately. If you're a college freshman, it's OK to include a few significant things from high school, but if you're a sophomore or older, high school experiences really aren't relevant—stick to college activities. If you don't have a lot of recent work experience, concentrate on your skills, the relevant classes you're taking, and any volunteer or internship experiences you've had—even if you haven't been paid, these activities certainly count.

If you choose the functional format, instead of listing your work experiences you'll list your skills. Group them in appropriate categories, such as "Business Skills" and "Writing Skills." Under Business Skills, for example, you could list: "Proficient in most major software applications; have sales experience; trained students to work at a help desk." Under Writing Skills you might include "Wrote column for college newspaper; wrote master's thesis on the media's influence on social issues."

Whichever format you follow, you should end your résumé with other relevant experiences, activities, and honors. For example, any leadership experience you have would be important to include for nearly any internship application. Language skills are especially important for international internships or working or studying abroad. You should also list such things as membership in the photography club if you're applying for a photo-journalism opportunity and being the recipient of a Regents Scholarship or other academic award.

As you prepare your résumé, give yourself plenty of time to perfect it; rushed work always shows. Be clear and precise in your writing, and put everything in the right place. Also be sure you state any special interests. For instance, if you're applying to the State Department for an international internship, instead of saying that you'd like to be placed in Europe, say that you'd like to be placed in Paris or Krakow or wherever it is you're hungering to go. Being too general may lose you your dream position.

Once you've got everything nailed down, have someone read your résumé to see if anything's missing or to catch any mistakes; like every document in your application package your résumé should be clean and error free. Let your reader know exactly which position you're applying for so he or she can see if your wording and information are a match. If you're a student and want an objective opinion, ask an advisor or counselor at your internship office or career center; one of your professors; or a professional editor, proofreader, or résumé writer. Your career center may also hold résumé writing workshops. If you're not a student, a colleague, career coach, or professional writer or editor should have good advice. But we don't recommend that you use one of the generic résumé models or forms available online—it won't allow you to target your specific audience.

Here are two examples of internship-winning résumés.

SAMPLE 3: RÉSUMÉ

Will N. Tern   intern@mailaccount.com
5050 Experience Street
Sherman Oaks, CA 91043   888-867-5309

EDUCATION
University of California at Los Angeles
Expected graduation: June 2006
Bachelor of Arts in Economics—accounting minor
Cumulative GPA: 3.55/4.00. Dean's List, Honors

Ivy Business School, Boston, Massachusetts   June 2004
Summer Business Management Program
- Participated in class discussions on current business management practices and business ethics
- Analyzed case studies for use in study groups, to debate ideas, and to suggest improvements for business models

WORK EXPERIENCE
Argent Financial, Valley Village, California   Summer 2004
College Intern
- Involved in trending and forecasting for different divisions, products, and clients to determine the largest sector of consumers and predict their future consumption based on present trends
- Analyzed daily productivity reports to increase efficiency of staff operations
- Assisted senior management in developing a detailed operations manual for the financial services division

Benchmark Media, Los Angeles   Spring 2004
Marketing Intern
- Researched the social and economic attributes that influence young adults' tastes and preferences as consumers
- Applied marketing strategies to advertising using public benches as innovative outdoor exposure for multiple clients

- Prepared detailed results reports using *Excel* and *Word* spreadsheets to update clients on their marketing campaign

Dortoir Residence Hall, UCLA   2001–2002
Program Assistant
- Arranged for professors and staff to deliver presentations to residents on a wide variety of topics
- Provided peer counseling (listening and referring) for residents and responded appropriately in emergency situations
- Became knowledgeable about on-campus and community resources to refer students appropriately

EXTRACURRICULAR ACTIVITIES
Alpha Beta Gamma Fraternity, UCLA   2002–present
Fund-Raising Coordinator
- Research and identify possible fund-raising opportunities to maximize money raised for charity
- Implemented an event that increased donations by 15% and helped raise money for the Valley Community Center (Valley City, California)

Student Business Society, UCLA   2001–2003
Corporate Relations Director, Public Relations Committee
- Provided individuals with information and opportunities necessary for success in career development
- Performed corporate outreach and arranged six events for students to interact with business professionals
- Performed community service by providing mentorship to UCLA students interested in business

Investissement Banque, New York City, New York   June 2003
Future Leaders Program Participant
- Entered competitive program aimed at teaching the basics of investment banking as well as about other careers in finance

SKILLS
- Proficient using Microsoft *Word,* Microsoft *Excel, Access,* and Internet browsers (*Netscape* and *Explorer*)
- Fluent in oral and written Spanish

SAMPLE 4: RÉSUMÉ

Will N. Tern   intern@mailaccount.com
5050 Experience Street
Riverside, CA 99999   888-867-5309

EDUCATION
University of California, Los Angeles   Expected graduation: June 2006
Bachelor of Science in Political Science; International Relations minor
Cumulative GPA: 3.78

Course Work: International politics, foreign policy decision making, government and politics in post-Communist Russia, advanced international relations theory, social statistics, and honors composition

Independent Research Project: Wrote a twenty-eight-page report titled "Apathy among 18- to 25-Year-Old Voters." Interviewed twenty-six subjects and researched current periodicals covering educational, economic, and social issues.

SKILLS
- Excellent oral and written communication skills; proven ability to work in a team setting
- Fluent in spoken and written Farsi, conversational ability in Spanish
- Proficient using Microsoft *Word, Excel, PowerPoint,* and *Outlook*; familiar with HTML and Java
- Knowledge of advanced statistics and research methods

EXPERIENCE
Collegiate Democrats
Vice President, UCLA Chapter, 2003–2004
- Facilitated meetings, prepared agenda, scheduled speakers, and ensured adherence to parliamentary procedure
- Planned and organized successful events, including Rock the Vote Day; secured event location, three local bands, and five food vendors for event attended by over 200 students and resulting in 111 new voter registrations

- Handled all correspondence with the press, alumni, and community supporters

State Senator Dean Baldwin Re-election Campaign
Volunteer, Riverside, California, 2004
- Contacted local community groups to arrange speaking engagements for Senator Dean Baldwin
- Called constituents to inform them about the issues and the candidates that would be on the upcoming ballot
- Created database of volunteers' names, contact information, times available, and specials skills

Campus Coffee Connection
Head Barrista, Westwood, California, 2001–2003
- Trained and scheduled staff of ten barristas and nightly performers
- Implemented and hosted Wednesday Night Open Mic programs; increased revenue for traditionally slow evening by 20%
- Created publicity materials and signage for weekly events that resulted in larger audiences than in previous year

ACTIVITIES
Collegiate Democrats, member, 2001–present
- Los Angeles Literacy Center, volunteer reading assistant, 2002–2003
- Intramural Co-Ed Softball, team manager, 2002–2003

HONORS AND AWARDS
- Student Organization Officer of the Year, 2004
- National Student Success Scholarship Recipient, 2002–2003
- Dean's List recognition

The Statement of Interest

Sometimes in lieu of a cover letter or a writing sample, a potential employer will ask for a statement of interest. This fairly short piece of writing gives you the opportunity to describe your interest in and motivation for applying for the particular internship or other option. Somewhat like the personal statement that accompanies college and graduate school applications, the statement of interest is a way for employers to learn a bit more about you and for you to tell them how your background and experiences make you the best choice for the job.

Statements of interests are generally fairly informal and usually not longer than a page or two. But they can be critically important—some companies and agencies, including the Department of State, regard them as one of the most significant parts of an application—and they're an excellent way to match an applicant's interests and qualifications to the right opening.

When you write a statement of interest, start out with your goal for the opportunity: Are you looking for real-world experience in an area of study, to travel and learn more about a particular part of the world, to improve your language skills, to try a new career path? Be specific to the internship. For example, you might say:

> I am looking for an internship position that will allow me to get practical experience in my major area of interest, marine biology. I believe that by interning at your center, I will gain skills that my classroom study can't provide as well as a better understanding of what a career in marine biology might be like.

Go on to provide all the evidence that you've got the perfect qualifications. You might say:

> In addition to my courses in all facets of marine biology, I work as a volunteer at my college's marine rescue center and have assisted one of my professors with her research on manatees. I believe my

strong interest in this field and my enthusiasm for understanding and protecting marine life make me a great candidate for your exciting internship.

A statement of interest can include anything you feel is relevant to the particular opening. This can be related academic courses you've taken, personal experiences, and skills and talents you possess. The particular organization may also make requests you should be sure to fulfill. For example, the U.S. Department of State asks interns to include in their statements any specific disadvantages they may have overcome and whether or not they're a continuing student.

While this essay doesn't need to be long, it does need to be well written and free of errors. It also needs to be positive and strong; this is one time you need to toot your own horn and emphasize how capable and qualified you are. Keep working on your statement until you think it's just right, and then have someone with good communication skills critique and proof it.

Following are an example of a strong statement of interest and a winning personal statement for graduate school application.

SAMPLE 5: STATEMENT OF INTEREST

Sunset at Chaophraya was one of my favorite movies when I was a little girl. The story of the love between a Japanese solider and a Thai peasant girl became my first encounter with images of Japan. My fascination with the movie sparked my interest in Japanese culture. At the age of nine, I asked my father to find me a Japanese tutor. Masako, a Japanese graduate student living in Thailand, where I lived, became my Japanese teacher. Each week, Masako taught me Kanji characters and used simple vocabulary words to speak to me in Japanese. I helped her make a few Japanese and Thai dishes, and during dinner she would show me pictures of her family in Japan. My initial contact with the Japanese culture created my curiosity about different cultures and languages.

My family moved to the United States when I was ten years old. During my junior year of high school, I participated in a study-abroad program that sent me halfway around the world to live with a Spanish family of bread bakers. My love of the Spanish language grew, and I came home understanding more about the world. Last year, I lived, studied, and worked in Latin America. The opportunity to live abroad allowed me to immerse myself in Latin American cultures and broaden my knowledge of cultures around the world. I was also able to form close and personal relationships with people from those cultures. Their willingness to share their lives with me left me with a profound feeling for their country. My experiences showed me that only by living in a different country can one truly learn about another's culture.

The international experiences that I have had reaffirmed my desire to become a United States Foreign Officer. As a graduating senior, I am continuing my preparation to attend a graduate school in international affairs. My unique experiences in Spain and Latin America have given me the opportunity to understand the culture in only two areas of the world, and I believe that the JET program will continue to expand my horizons and allow me to become part of a cultural exchange with the Japanese people. Teaching English would allow me to share my stories and be an influence on students as well as a receiver of their culture and ideas.

As a sophomore at the University of California at Los Angeles, I was an active tutor of a second-grade student at a local elementary school. The shy girl uttered few words during our sessions together, but her simple paintings spoke volumes about how she perceived the environment around her. It is the connection I felt with my student that encourages me to continue being a teacher.

The JET program will combine my two passions: living abroad and teaching. A year spent in Japan will allow me to learn about the Japanese culture and see the world through the perspectives of the Japanese people. Teaching English to young Japanese students will allow me to become close to students and interact with them in a way that is rewarding and meaningful.

Although the movie *Sunset at Chaophraya* introduced me to beautiful images of Japan, it was my Japanese tutor, Masako, who developed my interest in her culture. The bond we had as student and teacher enabled both of us to learn—I learned Kanji and she learned about Thailand. I hope to re-create this kind of personal bond by being a JET teacher in Japan.

SAMPLE 6: PERSONAL STATEMENT

I grew up in Long Beach, California, the most ethnically diverse city in America. People of countless perspectives and backgrounds developed my worldview of looking beyond borders and past stereotypical lines. Cross-cultural exchange enriched nearly every aspect of my daily life, while urban violence forced an early introduction to social tensions and disparities. My loving family brought balance to this equation and helped me discover my passion for foreign study. During my junior year in high school, I was an exchange student and lived outside of Tokyo, and the shift into Japan's homogeneous society brought my multicultural upbringing into focus for the first time. Witnessing today's prosperous U.S.–Japan partnership contrasted against visible remnants of World War II, I saw the effects of cooperation and conflict on a global scale parallel to the results of cultural synergy and gang violence in my home town. By the time I entered the University of California at Los Angeles, my childhood exposure to diversity combined with my experiences abroad to motivate a deep-rooted academic interest in world politics and a professional desire for contributing to the study of international relations.

UCLA afforded me a uniquely international undergraduate education. With the support of faculty and research/travel grants, my classrooms extended far beyond Los Angeles. I studied politics and economics in the United Kingdom, France, Holland, and twice in Japan. Two of my most vivid memories abroad are of delivering a speech at the architecturally astounding Parliament Building in Budapest and laying a wreath on behalf of Americans in a ceremony at the Atomic Bomb Memorial in Hiroshima. My participation in over forty conferences in the United States and overseas involved organizing seminars, presenting original research, and meeting numerous academics, CEOs, diplomats, and heads of state.

It was awe inspiring to meet luminaries such as the Hungarian president and Japanese prime minister, but in retrospect it seems even more valuable to have made lasting connections with young people like myself, whose dreams and aspirations outweighed their educational or professional expertise. I have friends who resisted Milosevic's rule in Yugoslavia, debated the fate of Chechnya in Russia, and advocated democracy inside of China. My contact with such extraordinary students forged my optimism for multilateral cooperation and my concept of the serious challenges that exist for human security. International exchange defined my undergraduate years, because rather than just listen to the speeches of influential leaders, I asked them questions face to face; rather than just read about sweatshops and refugee camps, I saw them with my own eyes; and rather than just rely on CNN's cameras, I garnered insights from an international network of students who discussed the stories behind the headlines. These intense experiences, spanning the globe from New York to Beijing, energized me to apply my studies and push the boundaries of my undergraduate curriculum.

Combining seemingly disparate interests, I strove to incorporate a minor in mathematics with my study of political science by utilizing game-theoretic methods in several of my papers. But my most rewarding academic challenge at UCLA was writing a 120-page senior thesis identifying Theater Missile Defense (TMD) as the central issue in East Asian affairs for addressing key security questions persisting from the Cold War. I presented my research on several occasions; the most outstanding event was the Harvard Project for Asian and International Relations in Singapore, where I was honored to speak alongside professors and diplomats and discuss my conclusions with the president of Singapore. Completing an undergraduate thesis embodied the most relevant preparation for my graduate study, solidifying my desire to pursue research on the U.S.-Japan alliance, U.S.-China diplomatic and economic relations, and the question of Taiwan's international status.

In the same way that my thesis increased my academic proficiency, my internships and student leadership enhanced practical skills essen-

tial for achieving a Ph.D. Working with a Japanese foreign ministry official in residence at the RAND Corporation, I translated theoretical con-
cepts into policy analysis, culminating in two presentations on Korean
politics and Japanese military strategy. As an intern at the Henry L.
Stimson Center for International Security in Washington, D.C., I worked
with visiting scholars from Japan and China, conducting research for
policy briefings. From interviewing specialists at the Pentagon and State
Department, including then-Defense Secretary Cohen, I developed an
aptitude for professional interaction and sharpened my ability to for-
mulate questions that get to the crux of complicated international
issues.

As president of the UCLA Regents Scholar Society (RSS), I sought to
redefine a loosely structured group that met once a term for an ice
cream social into an extensive student-run academic and service organization. I learned that communicating a vision for an organization de-
mands initiative, careful planning, and knowledge of resources and that
realizing this vision requires tenacity, flexibility, and interpersonal skills.
RSS became one of the most active groups on the UCLA campus, facili-
tating forums for discussion with Nobel Prize winners and political fig-
ures and supplying talented students with a vehicle for giving back to
the community. I will apply the skills cultivated during these internships
and student leadership experiences toward completing a dissertation
and strengthening the academic foundation of my future career.

My primary goal is to be a university professor, engaging in research and teaching in international security, political economics, and
East Asian regional studies. I will also look to participate in the policy-
consultant and think-tank communities. These aims require training
within a political science program equipped with several of the nation's
best international relations scholars at an institution that can offer a
broad-based intellectual experience characterized by substantive interaction among students. The Department of Government at Harvard not
only has the resources and faculty expertise to advance my education
but offers an environment of study that draws from the Harvard community's international reach. A doctorate is essential to my efforts for
making a wide contribution to political science and a positive impact on

the study and practice of American foreign policy. I believe I can bring
my best to the table at Harvard while pursuing a Ph.D. to obtain the analytical tools and educational experience necessary for realizing my professional goals.

References and Letters of Recommendation

While neither references nor letters of recommendation are materials
you need to write, some potential employers will ask you for them.
The important thing here is to double-check which they're asking for
and supply them with the right information. References are people
who can vouch for you and your abilities, so you just need to choose
two or three people who know you well and supply their names and
contact information with your application. One caveat: Ask the
people ahead of time if it's OK for you to use them as references, because it's likely the organization will call or e-mail these people to see
what they have to say about you.

Letters of recommendation are exactly that—you need to contact
several people who have positive opinions of you and ask them to
write and send in a letter strongly recommending you for the opening. For both references and letter writers, think about professors,
colleagues in managerial positions, and leaders who have overseen or
worked with you on volunteer, research, or other relevant activities—
people who know you've got the right stuff.

Acing the Interview

If your stellar application materials have won you an interview, you've
taken a giant leap toward winning the internship. Now to make the
next big leap—acing the interview.

An interview is a key part of the application process. While you
can accomplish a lot on paper, you can do even more face-to-face: You
can project your enthusiasm, go into detail about your qualifications,
and find out what you need to know to decide if the opening is for

you. Yes, that's right, in an interview you not only answer a potential employer's questions but ask your own questions too.

How should you prepare for an interview? How is one likely to go? The following tips and advice, from interns and employers alike, should help you put your best self forward and score big.

How to Prepare

Because the interview is so important and because competition for many internships is fierce, you'll need to do some homework ahead of time to make sure it goes well.

Know What The Company or Agency Is All About. When you did your research to track down exciting internship possibilities, you probably learned a bit about the organization's products and services, company culture, mission, and other important information. Study that again, and check the company's Web site or marketing materials for additional or more current information. Also speak to previous interns if you haven't done so already. Knowing as much as you can about the company will help you answer a lot of the questions the interviewer might ask. It will also make you stand out as someone who's really interested in the position and took the initiative to dig deep.

Think about What You Want to Gain from the Experience. In addition to learning as much as you can about the company, take some time to think about what *you* hope to get from the internship. It can be general benefits (the opportunity to experience a new culture) or more specific skills or experiences (to improve editing skills, learn how to light product photos, practice a language, see what it's like to work in a public defender's office before you apply to law school). By knowing what you really want, you can determine from the answers you get to your questions if the position will help you reach your goals.

Understand Your Contribution. After thinking about what you hope to get, think about what you would bring to the position. It's likely an interviewer will ask you what you feel your strengths and skills are, and it's important to have them in mind so you can readily answer the questions. As in your written materials, don't be shy—you may be a modest person, but if you don't point out what a great intern you would be, the person interviewing you may never know.

Do a Mock Interview. If it's been a while since you've interviewed for a position, if you've never been interviewed, or if you just want to polish up your skills, it's a good idea to take part in a mock interview. If you're a student, your internship office or career center will probably hold these on a regular basis or will arrange for you to do one; a number of campus groups, such as UCLA's Asian Pacific Society and Latino Business Association, also help with mock interviews. If you're out of school, contact your alumni association to set one up with an alum in the appropriate field. Going through a practice interview will give you a sense of what the real thing will be like, give you time to put together strong answers and decide on the questions you want to ask, and calm the jitters you might be feeling because you're unfamiliar with what an interview is like.

Check Out the Logistics. As Woody Allen said, 80 percent of success is showing up—you've got to know where you're going and how to get there on time. If you've never been to the interview site before, locate it on a map or get directions on a Web site such as Mapquest or Yahoo, or call the organization to find out how to get there. You may even want to do a trial run to make sure you can find it and to see how long it takes to travel there. Parking is another issue: Ask someone at the company if there's visitor parking. If not, ask if you'll need to find street parking or a parking garage and then ask for recommendations. The key thing here is not to be late to the interview; you definitely don't want to start out by not handling the first assignment: showing up on time. Especially if your appointment is in the early morning or late afternoon, give yourself at least ten or fifteen minutes extra for bad traffic, full parking lots, or getting lost on unfamiliar streets.

Think Ahead. The night before the interview, decide what you're going to wear (recommendations are given later). Make sure it's all in good condition—clean, pressed, and with no rips or missing buttons—and lay it out to save time in the morning. Also gather any materials you're going to bring: anything the company asked for, an extra copy of your résumé or statement of interest in case the original was mislaid, directions, and the phone number in case you're unavoidably delayed. Then, get a good night's sleep; don't stay up till 2:00 A.M. if you need to be rested and alert for an 8 A.M. interview. Be sure to eat a good breakfast in the morning. You don't want to feel sick or faint, and you don't want to be embarrassed by a squawking stomach. (One caution here: Don't drink too much tea or coffee, it might make you jittery or require frequent trips to the restroom!) As you head into the interview, try to relax your neck and shoulders. Then take a deep breath—and put on that winning smile.

How to Look and Act

Looking businesslike and presenting yourself professionally can do a lot to help you land the internship. Not only will it make you feel confident and comfortable in the surroundings but it will show the interviewer that you're taking the opportunity seriously, that you're up to the responsibilities you'd be given, and that you'd fit in well with the company culture and environment.

Even if you're interviewing for an opening at a creative company, such as an advertising agency, where the typical attire might be pretty casual, it's best to dress up rather than down for your interview. That means a suit or a sports jacket and tie for men, a dress or suit for women (if you wear a dress or skirt, make sure it's not too short; try sitting down in it before you decide to wear it). If you're interviewing at a large corporate office, lean toward the more formal end; if everyone there wears a suit, you want to be dressed accordingly. If you're a student and your entire wardrobe consists of jeans and T-shirts, borrow something suitable from a friend or family member so you look as well as sound the part.

During the interview, you also want to act professionally. The interviewer not only will assess your skills and background but will see how you express yourself, how you interact with him or her, how confident you are. If you're nervous, try not to show it. Give the interviewer a firm handshake when you meet, and smile as you introduce yourself in a clear voice. As you talk, be aware of what you're doing; don't drum your fingers on the table, fidget in your chair, or swing your foot back and forth. Try to keep a pleasant expression on your face, and be friendly but not overly chatty. Look the interviewer in the eyes as you speak, and show your genuine interest in what he or she says; be sure never to act bored or superior. When the interview is over, shake hands again and give the person your sincere thanks.

Multiple Interviews. If your interview goes well, you'll sometimes be asked to come in for another one. Some organizations have a two- (or more) step process. For example, if you do well in an initial meeting with one interviewer, you might be asked to interview again with a committee or several employees of the organization. This type of more informal meeting lets people get to know you a little better and find out what you might be like to work with.

Alan, for example, went through a several-day-long interview period. Before his first interview with a public accounting firm in Los Angeles, he was invited to a social night for all the potential interns and a number of employees. Then he had a one-on-one interview at company headquarters, which he aced. Next, he was invited again to company headquarters for a four-hour-long meeting. For the first hour, he and the other candidates were treated to a fancy lunch with several partners and managers. Then, for three additional hours, all the candidates were evaluated on their ability to cooperate, lead, and problem solve based on their performance in several specially designed games. After that, there were two dinners and an LA Kings hockey game! Though he had to be on his toes for all of it, Alan was prepared. And he ended up winning a coveted summer internship.

If you meet with more than one interviewer or staff member, remember to shake each of their hands when you arrive and when you leave. If no one comes right up to introduce you, take the initiative and do it yourself. Also, remember that all the above rules apply no matter how many people are in the room with you.

How to Answer Questions

Interview questions can run the gamut from those asking for facts, such as what your major is and what your computer skills are, to those used to determine how you might react in a particular situation. If you've researched the company and spent time thinking about your goals, you'll easily be able to answer any question that links your interests and the internship position, such as "Why would you like to intern with our company?" Situational questions, such as "What would you do if X happened?", may take a little more thought. The key, though, is to always focus on your strengths. For example, if you were applying for a teaching position in a foreign country and the interviewer asked what you would do if a child had a medical emergency, you should answer to the effect that your skill with the language and your classes in psychology would enable you to determine the problem, calm the child, and call for help.

Ahead of time you can think about and prepare answers to several questions you're likely to be asked, such as, "Tell me something about yourself" and "What are your career goals?" Again, focus on your strengths as you provide the information. See "Ten Top Interview Questions" on p. 126 for more samples.

It's, of course, impossible to know every question you'll be asked. But whichever questions come your way, remember you don't have to blurt out an answer, you can take a moment of two to pull together your thoughts. You should also remember to speak clearly and calmly and as you normally do; there's no need to pile on industry slang or use fancy vocabulary. The bottom line is, no one expects you to be Shakespearean—you'll make a great impression if you're just yourself.

TEN TOP INTERVIEW QUESTIONS

- Tell me something about yourself.

- What are your career goals?

- Why would you like to intern at our company?

- What will you bring to the internship?

- What are your strengths? What are your weaknesses?

- What course work, jobs, activities, or interests qualify you for this position?

- Give me an example of a time you displayed strong leadership skills.

- Tell me about a time when you worked as part of a team to reach a common goal.

- Tell me about one of your proudest accomplishments.

- If you could have any job, what would it be?

Questions to Be Sure to Ask

In addition to the types of questions mentioned earlier, there's an important one that almost every interviewer will ask: "Do *you* have any questions?" The answer to that one is simple: yes! Always have a few questions in mind both to come across as serious about the opening and to find out all the things you want to know.

What should you ask? Your questions will depend on the company and what's important to you. But here are several possibilities to kick-start your own list:

- **What would my duties and responsibilities be?** You want your tasks clearly defined, and you want to hear that you won't be spending the entire time doing busy work or grunt work.

- **Will I earn an hourly wage or receive a stipend?** If the internship is paid, find out what you'll make. But remember that if it's unpaid, the experience and the education may be more important in the long term.

- **How many hours will I work?** Find out the amount of time you'd be expected to be on the job, including the possibility of overtime or working on weekends or at night. Try not to commit to more than you can handle—the employer might reduce the time requirement if you ask.

- **Are there special experiences your company offers interns?** Find out if you'll be able to sit in on high-level meetings, meet visiting dignitaries, or work on challenging projects.

- **Will I receive training for the position?** Some internships will have a formal, structured training period, while others will be more learn as you go.

- **What is appropriate work attire?** Find out if it's dresses and suits or something more casual. You can also ask if there are dress-down Fridays. Knowing what you'll need to wear ahead of time can save you from spending money on clothes you won't need.

- **Will my work be reviewed at regular intervals or not until the end of the internship?** Some companies will have a fairly structured assessment process, whereas others will check in with their interns only from time to time. Many will also have an exit evaluation when the internship is over.

- **When will I hear if I'm being offered the internship?** Before the interview ends, ask your interviewer how soon you'll be notified if you've gotten the position. This will help with your planning, and give you a date when you can call the company if no one has gotten back to you.

How to Do a Phone Interview

If you apply for an internship or other option in another part of the country or the world, it's possible you'll be asked to interview by phone if you can't be interviewed at the organization's site. If you're scheduled to talk by phone, the information given earlier (except, of

THE FIVE BIGGEST INTERVIEW MISTAKES

According to a survey taken by www.careerbuilder.com, there are five big mistakes that many internship candidates make:

- **They say the wrong things.** The most common mistake that interviewees make is that they communicate badly. They either talk as if they were speaking from a script, give one-word answers, swear, go on and on about their personal problems, are much too candid (such as saying they're not a morning person), or spend the time complaining.

- **They don't prepare and they behave inappropriately.** Many interviewees don't research the company, so they aren't able to answer important questions. Others don't pay attention to the questions or try to bluff their way through them. Still others forget common sense and common courtesy—like taking calls on their cell phone during the interview. And others let their nerves get the best of them and bite their nails or need to run off to the restroom.

- **They display the wrong attitude.** Many candidates either brag or name-drop, whereas others show no interest whatsoever.

- **They have an unprofessional appearance.** Unprofessional includes everything from slouching in the chair to wearing a short skirt or too-tight pants to having dirty fingernails to sporting pink hair.

- **They're dishonest.** Some candidates exaggerate wildly, and some even forget to mention their little run-in with the law.

course, for tips that relate to your appearance) still applies: Talk calmly and clearly, think ahead about possible questions, and develop a list of questions of your own. Being on time is still important; you won't have to travel anywhere, but you will still need to be at the phone at the scheduled time. In fact, be there a little early, and make certain no one will interrupt you or pick up an extension while you're talking. And be sure that there won't be any noise to compete with your voice. Tell all housemates or colleagues that you need a whole lot of silence—no loud discussions, no music playing. Close your door if you can, and post a sign saying "Quiet, Please!" At the end of the interview, thank the interviewer for his or her time.

Acing the Follow-Up

You sent in a great application. You were spectacular in your interview. But while you deserve a big pat on the back, you're not finished yet; now you need to complete the process with a few final, very important steps.

Record Interview Information

As soon as possible after your interview, get out some paper or go to the computer and record the name, title, and company of the person who interviewed you; if you end up having several interviews, this will help you remember who's who. Also note the interview date. Then write a few lines about the key issues you discussed: what your responsibilities would be; if you would be paid; and any promises that were made, such as attending specific conferences or having the opportunity to spend time with the president of the company. Making these kinds of notes will help you in two ways: First, you'll remember the name of the person you need to send a thank-you note to and, second, if you accept the internship and it doesn't go the way you were told it would, you'll have a record of what was discussed and agreed to in your interview. Armed with that information, you can bring it to your supervisor's attention and ask that you be given the responsibilities or opportunities you had expected.

Thank Your Interviewer

Right after your interview—a face-to-face meeting or one done by phone—take a few minutes to compose a thank-you note to send to your interviewer. E-mail won't cut it here; it's too easy for e-mails to be missed or deleted, and they're often too informal. Write your note on a real piece of paper.

In your note, thank your interviewer (spelling his or her name correctly) for taking the time to meet with you and provide details about the opportunity. If you met with several people at the organization, you need to write to only the lead person, but ask that person to thank the others for you. Then, before adding "sincerely yours" and your signature, tell the interviewer you enjoyed meeting him or her and re-emphasize your interest in the opening. An enthusiastic, well-worded, handwritten thank-you note will bring you front and center in the interviewer's mind and distinguish you from the other candidates.

Thank Your Supporters

If other people helped you with any part of the application process— from reviewing your cover letter to taking part in a mock interview— now would be a great time to thank them, too. Give them a call, write them a note, but let them know you appreciate their help. You can also let them know that you've completed the application process. Now all you have to do is wait for the offers to pour in!

A FEW FINAL TIPS

- If you're mailing in your application, submit all the materials in one envelope.

- In your résumé, cover letter, and any other writing samples, avoid using slang or profanity. If you want to include acronyms, be sure to note what the letters stand for, in case the reader isn't familiar with the organization you're referring to.

- Always use action words, rather than the passive voice, in all of your writing, to give your writing a confident, energetic feel.

- Proofread, proofread, proofread!

- Check and double-check deadlines—get your application in on time.

- Focus all parts of your application on the specific organization; don't use the same materials for all the internships you apply for.

- Remember that you're not in this alone; get the help you need from counselors, advisors, colleagues, and former interns.

Chapter 9
Make the Most of Your Time on the Job

Congratulations—you won the internship! All your hard work and persistence paid off, and you're about to embark on a brand-new adventure. We hope it's a positive experience, and we're certain it will be a valuable one.

But all internships, of course, are not alike, and the success you have with yours will depend on many variables. However, every internship experience has one deciding factor in common: the intern—you—need to do everything you can to make it enjoyable and fulfilling.

To a great extent, your internship will be what you make of it. Your attitude, work ethic, energy, and desire to learn will play critical roles in how well your internship goes and how much you benefit from it. While you need to have a positive attitude from the start, you can't expect that a great experience will just be delivered to you. You need to work hard and take advantage of every opportunity.

To help you make the most of your time on the job, follow these tips, gathered from former interns, employers and supervisors, and internship center staff.

Have Realistic Expectations

Although you're probably excited about the position you've won—and you should be—it's important to keep your feet planted firmly on the ground. You may be interning at the White House, or Dream-Works, or a senator's office, or a major publishing firm, all of which sound pretty glamorous; but you shouldn't expect to jump right into a glamorous assignment. Eventually, after you gain some experience and expertise, you *may* be given opportunities that will thrill or inspire you. But, especially in the beginning, you need to realize that you'll be doing a lot of learning and adjusting. Keep in mind that you're a newcomer and probably the low person on the totem pole. Try not to expect too much so you don't set yourself up for disappointment.

David, an intern from New York University, described how keeping his expectations in check actually increased his job satisfaction. Before he began working at a health organization, he thought he would be spending a good deal of his time doing grunt work. When he found himself doing much more meaningful work, he experienced a strong feeling of making a difference.

Understand That the First Two Weeks Might Be Tough

Part of having realistic expectations is understanding that the first two weeks on the job might be especially challenging. That's because, wherever you're interning, everything will be new—from the office environment to the people you associate with to the work you'll be doing to the city or town or country you'll be living in. All of that newness might be disorienting; it might even make you unhappy or anxious. So try your best to stay calm and positive; once you have a week or two under your belt, you'll probably feel a lot more comfortable. One thing you can do to alleviate your concerns is to share them with a friend or colleague; it usually helps to tell all to a sympathetic listener. You can also see if you can arrange to visit your new office a day or two ahead of time to see the lay of the land and perhaps meet a few people. Often even a bit of familiarity makes the first few days a little less daunting.

Let Your Supervisor Know Your Strengths and Interests

If you haven't discussed this already, be sure to let your supervisor know which areas of the internship are the most important and intriguing to you. While you might think this would be pushy, it's really not; though it won't always happen, supervisors are generally willing to try to match some of your tasks to your particular strengths and interests. And how can they know what those are unless you tell them!

File and Copy with a Smile

Even if your supervisor sends a good deal of challenging work your way, you can still assume you're going to be doing a fair amount of filing, copying, data entry, coffee making, and other forms of busy work. Just about every organization has this kind of work to be done, so you'll be expected to pitch in. Fortunately, you probably won't be the only one doing these less-than-thrilling chores. In small offices especially, just about everyone is asked to wash the mugs and add more ink to the printer, but because you're there to help out the staff as well as learn more about the field, clerical and clean-up jobs will likely be part of your daily tasks. At UCLA, we ask employers to indicate in their internship descriptions approximately what percentage of the time students will be handling clerical or administrative work. It shouldn't be all of it, but it will be some.

One silver lining to keep in mind: The more willing you are to cheerfully do the grunt work, the more likely you'll be given much more stimulating responsibilities.

Ask to Have Your Responsibilities Spelled Out

If you had an interview, your responsibilities were probably laid out in general terms (and you should have those responsibilities recorded in your postinterview notes). But even if you had an interview, it's best to ask your supervisor on day one just what you'll be expected to do. As you talk, take good notes so you'll remember everything. If something isn't clear, be sure to ask questions until it is. And, if at all possible, ask to have your tasks given to you in writing. Many offices and agencies provide interns with written work plans so they can see the big picture for the entire internship period. Some work plans, such as the "Intern Work Plan" for the Heads Up! Network branch of the Head Start early childhood education program, on p. 136, include between-project recommendations for additional ways to learn.

Do More Than You're Asked to Do

Whatever your assignment, you want to do it as well as you possibly can. But if you finish it, and don't have another job to follow, don't just sit there and wait for something to come to you. Take the initiative and actively search out another project. Ask your supervisor for something new to tackle or if there's someone else in the office who's backlogged and needs a helping hand. Your supervisor will be happy that you've come to him or her (sometimes supervisors can't bring you new assignments because they're knee deep in their own), and you'll be thought of as someone with get up and go.

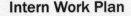

Intern Work Plan

Customer data management
- Make address changes to customer file from returned mail
- Create facilitator database
- Add the following to college list on Web site:
  - Number of credits
  - E-mail contact info
  - Academic level for which course is offered

Research funding sources for
- *HeadsUp! Math* re: WGBH TV
- *HeadsUp! Reading*
- *HeadsUp! Social Emotional*
- Network

Update Web site data
- Fix all eight to fourteen class materials for Web site

Data management
- Update programming database with *EchoStar* tape archive information
- Improve appearance of Welcome Kit
- Proofread materials, Web sites

Conference preparation
- Prepare/pack materials for conferences
- Make new shipping box for dish tripod

Customer support
- Once knowledgeable enough, answer toll-free phone calls and main box e-mails
- Hold the fort while team is in Anaheim at annual conference (April 19–23)

Get on-site experience at a range of Head Start programs
- Visit/volunteer at Higher Horizons Head Start
- Visit/volunteer at a less fortunate Head Start center

Process *HeadsUp! Reading* Continuing Education Units applications

Between projects, learn about the early childhood field and Head Start
- Attend intern orientation
- Visit Web sites, review materials provided by HeadsUp! team: Partnership for Reading, 0-3, ECS, NAS, Touchpoints, WGBH, PBS/Ready to Learn, others
- Attend meetings, hearings, conferences, and other events
- Meet with selected national Head Start staff
- Visit by phone or in person with selected early childhood staff

Other duties as assigned

By asking to do more, two interns who worked for the U.S. Department of Agriculture ended up doing something that had never been done before: developing a definition of processed food based on harmonized tariff codes. After learning the agricultural service trace extract software, the two applied their computer and Internet skills to make a significant contribution.

Put in Extra Hours if You Can

Most full-time internships, except for some in the media field, will have regular business hours, often a forty-hour week. But if you're asked to do some overtime, either on the weekends or during the evenings, it's a good idea to say yes if you can. Putting in a few extra hours, no matter when it is, will show your enthusiasm and flexibility and your willingness to help out when needed—and it will make your employer think you're a gem. As a bonus to you, it might give you the opportunity to take part in an exciting event that doesn't usually happen between nine and five. Joan, for example, who was interning at the White House, was asked to come in on a Saturday morning to help prepare for a press conference and ended up meeting and having her photo taken with the president.

Ask Questions, Ask for Help, Ask for More Responsibility

Though you may be on the bottom rung of the ladder, that doesn't mean you should be seen but not heard. If you need something clarified, ask for an explanation. If you can't handle a project on your own, let your supervisor know. If you want to take on something that's not part of your job description, ask if you can give it a try. By asking questions you can avoid making costly mistakes. And by asking for more responsibility you just might get it, adding greatly to your experience and making you even more valuable to the team.

Be Enthusiastic, But Not *Too* Enthusiastic

Even if you're spending a day updating addresses on a mailing list, try to do it with a smile. Employers are always pleased to have interns with a positive attitude; one of the biggest complaints employers have is that many interns don't show interest in what they're doing, and they usually prefer to help the more enthusiastic and involved interns move ahead. Showing interest in all your projects will make it likely you'll be given more meaty ones.

Remember, though, not to be overly enthusiastic or sugary sweet, that will turn employers off just as quickly. While employers want their interns to be bright, attentive go-getters, they don't want them to go overboard. Many former interns say that keeping a low profile, and working as part of a team, are keys to having a successful internship. Though you may have a special passion or cause related to the job, be tactful in how you pursue it. Try to strike a balance between taking initiative and pressuring others to follow your lead.

Don't Just Do It, Do It Well

If you're supposed to take phone messages, answer every call. But also be sure to be friendly and helpful, as well as obtain and write down all essential information. And if the call is important, let the intended recipient know. By doing a superior job on the smaller tasks, your supervisor will feel confident giving you greater responsibility. And by always going the extra mile, you'll get yourself noticed.

Network, Network, Network

Whether you're in a big organization or a small one, take every opportunity to get to know as many people as you can. Not only will this help you feel comfortable more quickly but it can also benefit you in many other ways. First, you'll probably find several friends to enjoy some nonoffice time with. Second, some of the people you meet now may be good contacts later. Bob, who interned with a sportswear company, made it a priority to meet every designer on the staff. Two years later, when he had graduated and was looking for a job, he called one of the designers and found that she was about to start her own line. The designer remembered Bob well and asked him to be part of her team.

A third reason to meet everyone you can is that one of those people might be willing to be your mentor. Mentors can give you advice and guidance, not only during your internship but as you continue down your career path. Someone who knows the ropes and takes a special interest in you and your goals can do wonders in helping you succeed.

Keep Confidential Information Confidential

Friendly conversation with office colleagues is encouraged, but if you deal with sensitive or confidential material, it shouldn't be talked about in the outside world. Especially in government agencies, such as the Department of State of your local congressman's office, and in companies where intellectual property is key, confidential matters are part of the daily fare, but you'll be expected to be discrete about them. Remember that the person behind you in the elevator or sitting at the next table in a restaurant could be a competitor or even a reporter. If people ask you for information about where you work, refer them to your supervisor if you don't know them or aren't sure what they're after.

Don't Look for Special Treatment

Because you're the new person, you'll probably be given some guidelines to follow and perhaps some special training. But interns generally aren't given special attention, they're expected to dig in, do their job, and fit in. Some supervisors will go out of their way to encourage, support, and instruct. But no supervisor is going to hold your hand. Supervisors have projects of their own and maybe even a crisis or two to handle. So they won't be inclined or have the time to work with you every minute of every day. While you should certainly go to your supervisor with problems or if you need questions answered or more work to do, aim on being as self-reliant as possible.

Learn to Use the Equipment

While it may seem like a no-brainer, it can be very important to learn to use the equipment. First of all, it's likely you'll be involved in photocopying or faxing or data entry in your work, and while you may know how to do that on your current office's or school's equipment, the machines where you're interning may operate completely differently. Second, it's an opportunity to learn how to use equipment and software you're not familiar with, which could come in handy at a future job or be a plus on your résumé. Ask a member of the office staff to show you how to operate the key pieces of equipment.

Communicate Effectively

To do your work as well as you can, you'll need to communicate with those around you. Whenever you're given an assignment, verify that you understand what's expected of you. When you go to a meeting, prepare ahead of time so you can say what you need to say. Establish a means of feedback so that you can learn what went right about a project and what needs to be improved. Be friendly, be direct, be clear, be accurate.

Matt, a senior from the University of Oregon, interned with a fairly large political organization. As part of his job, he had to respond to constituents' questions by phone and by letter. He also had to update information packets and articles and occasionally obtain copyright permission. Accurate, clear communication was critical to just about everything he did, so he learned to double-check his facts, keep a friendly attitude, take careful notes, and ask questions when he wasn't sure.

Follow through with Commitments

When you accept an internship, you accept all its parameters. That means you not only need to carry out the responsibilities you're given but you need to get to work on time, stay until closing, and respect all the office do's and don'ts. If you promised anything during the interview, such as being willing to work on alternate weekends or whenever needed, remember to willingly fulfill the obligation when the time comes.

Don't Be Afraid to Deal with Problems

Many interns feel that there's no way to fix an internship that's not going the way it was described, especially if it's unpaid. But you should always go to your supervisor about that or any other major issue. Supervisors can get caught up in their own responsibilities and not realize you're having difficulty. Or you may not be their first priority; in fact, some supervisors may not even be happy they were asked to manage an intern. But whatever the situation, your supervisor is still obliged to help you have a good experience. Just be sure to approach him or her politely, calmly, and intelligently.

If your problem is that you're not being given the work and the responsibility you were told you would have, ask your supervisor for a meeting. Referring to the notes you took after your interview, remind the person what was promised. If nothing changes after your talk, ask for a meeting with the head of the organization or someone at a high level. And if nothing changes after that, it's perfectly appropriate to leave. However, before you make the decision to quit, discuss it with a counselor or, if you're a student, the person who's monitoring your independent study. An objective ear may help you determine a way to solve the problem before taking drastic action.

Remember Your Goals

While you're doing your internship, it's a good idea to keep your goals for the experience in mind. Octavio, an intern at a medical foundation, advises making a list of your goals before you start the new position and checking them periodically to see how you're doing. If one of your goals was to learn what it takes to get a business off the ground, your list will remind you to network with people in several different departments. If another one was to experience living in a foreign country, your list will remind you to take more advantage of local events. Reminding yourself of why you chose this particular path will help you use it to the fullest extent.

Don't Ask for a Full-Time Job on the First Day

One of the reasons you took the internship may be that you hope you'll be asked to stay on permanently. But don't ruin your chances for that to happen by immediately asking for a full-time position. Internships and other options are designed to last for several weeks to several months, and employers generally want that time to assess your skills and learn more about you. It's possible that at the end of the internship you will be offered a full-time opening—you can bring it up yourself then, particularly in an exit or evaluation meeting—but jumping the gun may put the employer off. In fact, some employers might think you're not really interested in learning if you ask for a job before you understand its ins and outs. Asking too soon can work against you in another way: You might find that the field doesn't stir your passions after you've committed to coming onboard.

Take Advantage of Every Opportunity

Take advantage of opportunities on the job as well as those that surface beyond the office walls. In the office, take advantage of every chance to learn. If you're photocopying a document for a major new marketing push, ask the creators to tell you more about it and ask if you can provide any help. If new people join the team, go out of your way to meet them and find out what they do. Have lunch with employees as well as with other interns. Stay late or come in on the weekend if there's a chance to meet someone important in the field or be part of an exciting project.

Cherie, a junior from the University of California at Davis, interned at the National Women's Health Network in Washington, D.C. There she provided health-related information to many women and men who were trying to make important decisions about their care. After participating in the March for Women's Lives during her internship, she was offered the opportunity to write about the march from her perspective. While she was a bit nervous about taking it on, writing the article turned out to be important. "Not only did it make me feel trusted and responsible," Cherie said, "but it built my confidence that I could handle things in a professional manner."

Outside the office, take every opportunity to learn more about the area, the culture, and the people where you're living. Don't be a spectator, dive in and participate. See the local—and maybe not-so-local—sights. Eat the area specialties. Maybe try a home stay. If your supervisor or colleagues invite you to their home or an event, drop everything to go, then invite them to join you sightseeing; they'll probably love to be your tour guide. The idea is to learn and do and enjoy as much as possible. There's much more to a quality internship than just the nine to five.

Enjoy the Freedom and Flexibility That Comes with Being an Intern

Although you may wish that you were working as a full-time paid employee, there are lots of advantages to being an intern. Yes, you'll have assignments, but you won't need to accomplish a major feat month after month. And you may be able to get a taste of several departments instead of working in just one. An internship is a short-term learning experience, and with that comes a good deal of freedom and flexibility. If you take the initiative; stay open to people, processes, and perspectives different from your own; and maintain your sense of humor, your internship will most likely be a valuable and enlightening time.

Keep a Journal

Keeping a journal about important events is a great way to keep them fresh and to help you remember how you felt going through them. Journaling is also a wonderful way to learn from your experiences. To help you do all of that, you may want to start a journal as soon as you start looking for an internship. Recording the process you go through will not only prompt you to consider all the ways it affected you but might also inform others who follow (if you're in school, you might be able to post some of your thoughts on the internship center Web site for other students to read).

If you haven't been keeping a journal from day one, you may want to write in one during the course of your internship. In addition to having a special book in which to detail your experiences and express your emotions, you'll have a record of just what you did that you can use in your end-of-internship paper or for discussion during your exit evaluation. If you're traveling, studying, or teaching, either in the United States or abroad, a journal can be an especially important way to record your experience. Nick, from the University of California at Santa Cruz, kept not only a journal but a book of sketches to record his travels throughout the country.

Thank Your Supervisor at the End of the Internship

While a number of people may have helped you during your time as an intern, it's probably your supervisor who you've got to thank for showing you the ropes, explaining the details, and making your internship a valuable learning experience. Supervisors often go out of their way to help and educate their interns, so as your internship comes to a close, a major thank you is definitely in order. Actually, two are in order: an oral one delivered in person and a written one that the supervisor might want to keep in a file. Some interns also give their supervisors a small gift in appreciation, such as a coffee mug; students might like to give a mug or other gift that carries the name of their university.

Chapter 10
How to Know If You're on the Right Career Path—And What to Do If You're Not

If you've read through the previous chapters, you've seen how invaluable internships can be. On the experiential level, they stretch your boundaries, build your skills, increase your confidence, and open doors to opportunity. They also help you become more self-aware and more knowledgeable. And on a practical level, they help you find out if the field you intern in is one you want to pursue.

Doing an internship will give you real-world proof that you are, or aren't, on the right career path. Sanjay, for instance, who completed a ten-week internship in California Representative Nancy Pelosi's Washington, D.C., office, found that being in politics and serving the public was exactly what he wanted to do. He had thought this was the right direction for him, and the internship showed him that it was. Britney, on the other hand, interned at a financial institution, and though she was offered a full-time job at the end, she turned it down because the experience never challenged or excited her. She later did an internship at a public relations firm and found that this was the field where her passions lay.

After you've completed your internship, you'll certainly know whether or not you enjoyed the experience. But you may not be sure whether the field in which you interned or a particular position you learned about is truly your career dream. If the internship was negative, and you were completely turned off by the experience, you may be at a loss as to what to do next. Both of these situations can be addressed by focused thought and positive action.

Evaluating Your Experience

At the end of an internship, some evaluation steps may be required; others are important to take whether they're mandatory or not.

Writing Papers and Recording Your Thoughts

If you're a student, it's likely you'll be required to write and submit a paper about your experience to receive credit from the professor who sponsored you. The paper is often an assessment of what you learned, the skills you developed, and how the internship benefited you; the topic may also be one directly related to the internship field. Writing this paper—though it may seem like a huge chore with all the other things you need to do—is actually a great way to think about how you spent the internship period and what it meant to you.

Georgia, the University of California at Davis junior who interned for the HeadsUp! Network division of Head Start, was given the option of writing about any subject that interested her (her paper was required for the research seminar she took as part of her internship program). She chose to focus on a topic that was connected to her internship: the reauthorization of Head Start and the current administration's plan to move funding from the federal to the state level. While working on her paper, she was able to draw on her internship experiences as well as learn a lot more about the operation of an early-childhood educational program—an area filled with possibility for her future.

Sean, who interned in a congressman's Washington, D.C., office, had a research requirement as part of his school's program. Because the congressman he worked for was very involved with security issues, Sean chose to research and write a paper on steps the U.S. government is taking to improve security around the world. Writing the paper helped Sean realize that he had learned a great deal during his internship and helped him see that he could apply much of his knowledge in a future government capacity.

If you're asked to write a paper, you may be given specific points to discuss or the content may be completely up to you. But whatever the focus, use the opportunity to consider all the aspects of the experience (if you're not required to write a paper, it's a good idea to record your thoughts anyway; writing is a great method for expressing what you really feel and gives you something tangible to mull over). Use the journal you kept (see Chapter 9) to remind yourself and write about the different tasks you undertook, the people you met, skills you gained or improved, what challenged you, what you didn't enjoy at all, what sparked your day, what you had difficulty with, what you feel you learned. Your journal may also provide insights on an emotional as well as a practical level. After you get it all down, consider if what you said indicates a true interest in the field: Are you excited about it? Is it something you see yourself happily engaged in in the future? Was the job not exactly right but what you saw around you completely absorbing? Are you eager to apply what you learned in a related capacity?

It's also important to ask yourself if a job in the specific field would let you meet your career goals. If you'd like to travel or serve the public, would this type of work allow you to do that? If developing particular skills is something you want to achieve, would you be able to develop them in that position? Think back to why you wanted to do the internship and what you hoped to accomplish. Also consider whether or not the internship refocused your career goals, and if a job in the field will allow you to realize your new dreams.

In addition to writing a long paper (often twenty pages or more), students are generally asked to evaluate their internship for their internship center and future interns. This can be another excellent way to consider the experience—the reviews can be anonymous, so you can say exactly what you think. The evaluation (some schools ask interns to fill out a form, others require a two- to three-page paper) includes negatives and positives, what the student learned from the experience, and whether or not the student would recommend the internship to others. Evaluations are either retained in the internship office or posted on the center's Web site. If you put some real thought into this kind of "summing-up" paper, you'll not only help future interns in their selection process but get a good sense of how your experience affected you.

If you've completed a fellowship or other post-college-level program, you've probably had longer than the typical ten- or twelve-week internship period to assess your interest. This kind of longer-term thinking can be especially good in bringing clarity, since staying in a position for several months or even years gives you an in-depth look at it, beyond the exhilaration you often feel at the start of something new. Use the journal you've been keeping to help you zero in on what you've learned and how you feel about it. Because people doing fellowships and other longer-term programs are often offered a full-time job after the program ends, also ask yourself if continuing in the position would be a wonderful prospect or if moving on to something new would be more fulfilling.

Taking Part in an Exit Evaluation

Before your internship ends, it's important to go through an informational interview with your supervisor. This kind of final meeting will provide you with helpful feedback to add to your considerations. Your supervisor will probably set one up, but if he or she doesn't, ask

---

TEN TOP QUESTIONS FOR EVALUATING YOUR INTERNSHIP

- Would you want to do the same internship again?
- What would you change about the work to make it more interesting?
- Can you see yourself doing work in this field ten years from now?
- Was the work challenging?
- Did you learn new skills or improve existing skills?
- Were you excited to go to work in the morning?
- Did you like the environment?
- Were you comfortable with your co-workers?
- Do you wish the job had gone on longer or were you ready to leave?
- Did the work meet or exceed your expectations?

---

when a convenient time would be to meet. In the interview, ask your supervisor about the quality of your work and if he or she would recommend that you go into the field. If the answer is yes, find out more about what a career in the area might entail. For example, would you need a master's or a doctorate to advance? Would you need to spend some time in another location or abroad? What kind of additional skills would be helpful? Also ask your supervisor about how he or she got into the field, and if it's fulfilling and challenging. Ask anything that will help you with your decision-making process; prepare a list ahead of time and don't hold back.

An exit interview is also a great time to talk about future possibilities with the company. Your supervisor may use the interview to offer you a full-time job, but if that doesn't happen you can bring the subject up yourself. If you're not about to graduate, you can ask about the likelihood of being hired when you do graduate. An offer may not come through, but you can still get a sense of possibilities in the particular field.

If you won't be staying on, you can also ask your supervisor for a letter of recommendation. Then, when you're ready to apply for a full-time job, you'll have a glowing description of your work ethic, skills, and capabilities.

Turning a Negative into a Positive

While internships are great learning experiences, not all of them will be positive. There's definitely a chance that the field you thought was perfect will turn out to be boring or just completely different, in a negative way, from what you were expecting. It's possible that the job you thought would be a dream might actually be a nightmare.

If your internship was closer to a nightmare than a dream, your inclination might be to feel it was a waste of time. But that really isn't the case. In fact, finding the downside of a potential career can save you time and energy in the long run: avoiding additional classes in the wrong major and taking a job in the wrong field, which would eventually cause you to start over. An internship is invaluable for showing you you're on the right track, but it can be equally invaluable for showing you early on that you're on the wrong one.

The important thing with any internship is to be realistic—if you find the field doesn't interest you, breathe a sigh of relief that you found out sooner rather than later and start thinking in a new, positive direction. Here are some ways to do just that.

Talking It over with a Counselor

If your internship showed you that a change of plan is in order, a good way to begin that change is by arranging to talk to a counselor. If you're a student, a career center counselor should be a great source of help; if you're out of school, a private counselor or coach or your alumni association should have resources to guide you. Any experienced counselor will be able to help you evaluate your internship experience, to find both the pros and the cons, and then help you look into other areas.

Career center counselors may suggest that you consider other fields related to your major and have you read through books that detail specific jobs related to specific majors (for a few of these books, see the appendix). You can do this on your own, through the library or a bookstore, if you're no longer in school. There are literally thousands of job possibilities in many different fields, and sitting down with these types of resources will make you aware of them.

One thing to keep in mind is that you might actually like the field you tried, just not the particular position or department you learned about. For example, you might have interned in the customer service department of a government agency and not enjoyed it at all, but would actually be very happy working in the public affairs office of that type of agency. Think about what other positions are available in your original field of interest; set up meetings with people who work where you interned to find out more about what they do.

If something catches your interest—either a suggestion from a counselor, a career you uncover in your reading, or something you come up with on your own—start looking into it. Use the suggestions in Chapters 2 through 5 to help you in your search. Make sure that all possibilities intrigue and engage you; you want to find a career path that excites you, not just something to take the place of the one that didn't pan out.

Adding a Second Major

If you're a student and nothing related to your major grabs you, but something in a completely different field does, you may think that the only possibility is to switch to a new major and lose precious time and course credits. But this doesn't have to be the case. Rather than start over, you can add a second major. Particularly if you did your internship fairly early in your college career, you'll be able to fulfill the requirements and graduate with a degree that supports your new interest.

Talking It over with Others

In addition to speaking to a career counselor, you can also talk about your situation with a variety of other people: professors, visiting lecturers, alumni, office workers, and colleagues. Though it may not be apparent, there are numerous people in circles you might not have thought of who have valuable experiences to share with you. Tap into their knowledge; you might be surprised, and their insights might head you in a new and challenging direction. For example, a visiting professor recently surprised UCLA students by telling them that he didn't consider a law degree a necessity for going into politics. Students who had thought they would have to attend law school were instead encouraged to go to work for a senator or a congressman, where the professor felt they would obtain invaluable experience. Talking with someone familiar with a possible field of interest can save you time as well as get you focused in a positive direction.

Professors can also be great resources not only for their academic area of expertise but for other areas as well. Many professors either work in the private sector in addition to teaching or held a professional position before they became a teacher. Ask them what the work was like, the pros and cons, the potential. If you make an appointment and have a good list of questions at the ready, most professors will be happy to talk with you about your future.

If you're no longer in school, your alumni association can put you in touch with other alums in a variety of fields. You can also approach people in your community—in government, service work, business, whatever fields seem intriguing—to find out what their work is like on a day-to-day basis. Most people, even if you don't know them well, will be flattered that you asked and happy to talk. And if you arrange an interview with a prominent person in your area, you'll not only get your questions answered but probably get highly motivated as well.

Trying Something Completely Different

One way to leave behind a career that didn't thrill you is to head off somewhere entirely new—perhaps to a new city or new country. Volunteering or teaching through a program such as Teach America or the Peace Corps or simply traveling on your own is a great way to shake things up and give yourself a fresh start. Whether or not you think you might want to become a teacher, involving yourself with new people and new places will open doors and expand your horizons. It will also give you a chance to regroup and see what else is out there. If you started to explore your career possibilities early on, you'll have plenty of time to experience this option and consider any opportunities that emerge from it.

Doing Another Internship

If your first internship was pretty disappointing, you may want to get right back on the horse and do another one. If you've come up with a new career possibility, why not look right into it through a second internship? If you can fit it into your schedule, you could apply for a typical ten- or twelve-week position. But you could also look for a part-time opening that you could experience in addition to your classes. Nearly 66 percent of all students who do internships do two or more—some to deepen their skills in one area and to learn more about the industry, and some to check out several different fields. So keep in mind that, even though one internship didn't take you in a dream direction, the next one just might. Courtney, who did an internship with a motion picture company, found the experience not at all what she was looking for. By checking into a different communication field, she located another internship with a magazine. She found magazine work to be her true passion.

Rereading Your Journal

If you kept a journal during your internship—and we certainly hope you did!—reading it again closely may give you true insight into what it was you didn't enjoy and if there were any positive aspects on which you can build. It's possible that, lost in the depths of the overall disappointing experience, you've forgotten that one or two parts of the job actually produced sparks. Perhaps you commented in your journal about how great it was to write a press release, though most of your work was communicating face to face. Or how much you enjoyed helping a child or assisting in coordinating an event or helping develop an instant messaging system, though those weren't your main responsibilities. By rereading your journal or just sitting down and thinking long and hard about the entire experience, you'll discover keys to the work you like to do and the circumstances in which you enjoyed doing it.

Keeping Up Your Contacts

As you think about where you'd like to go next, try not to throw away all the equity you've already built. During your internship exit interview, be sure to remain polite and receptive, even if your experience was awful. Thank your supervisor for his or her time, and trade contact information with fellow workers you got to know. Though you may not have anything more to do with the company, the people you met there may be important in the future. They may be able to act as a reference for you when you apply for a full-time job, or they may know of interesting positions for you to look into. They may even move on to a different organization where you could do another internship or be part of the team. Be sure to stay in touch, through occasional phone calls, e-mails, or lunches, and keep their information handy so you can reach former colleagues when the time is right.

Appendix
Books and Publications

Works Cited in the Text

Basta, Nichols. *Major Options: The Student's Guide to Linking Majors and Career Opportunities during and after College.* New York: HarperCollins, 1991.

Brown, Sheldon S., and Mark Rowh. *Opportunties in Biotechnology Careers.* Lincolnwood, IL: NTC Contemporary, 2001.

Camenson, Blythe. *Great Jobs for Art Majors.* Lincolnwood, IL: VGM Career Books, 2003.

Collins, Joseph, Stefano Dezerega, and Zahara Hecksher. *How to Live Your Dream of Volunteering Overseas.* New York: Penguin Books, 2002.

DeGalan, Julie, and Stephen Lambert. *Great Jobs for English Majors.* Lincolnwood, IL: VGM Career Books, 2000.

Henderson, Harry. *Career Opportunities in Computers and Cyberspace.* New York: Facts on File, Inc., 2004.

Hirsh, Sandra, and Jean Kummerow. *Life Types.* New York: Warner, 1989.

Internship 2005. Princeton, NJ: Peterson's, 2005

Keirsey, David. *Please Understand Me II.* Chula Vista, CA: Prometheus Nemesis, 1998.

Landes, Michael. *The Back Door Guide to Short-Term Job Adventures: Internships, Extraordinary Experiences, Seasonal Jobs, Volunteering, and Working Abroad.* San Francisco: Ten Speed Press, 2002.

Oldman, Mark, *The Internship Bible.* New York: *Princeton Review, 2004.*

Rowh, Mark. *Great Jobs for Political Science Majors.* New York: McGraw-Hill, 2003.

Tieger, Paul D., and Barbara Barron-Tieger. *Do What You Are: Discover the Perfect Career for You through the Secrets of Personality Type:* Boston: Little, Brown, 2001.

General Directories

Internships. Princeton, NJ: Peteron's Guides, 2004.

Lands, Michael. *The Back Door Guide to Short-Term Job Adventures: Internships, Extraordinary Experiences, Seasonal Jobs, Volunteering, and Working Abroad.* San Francisco: Ten Speed Press, 2002.

Oldman, Mark and Samer Hamadeh. *The Best 106 Internships.* New York: Random House, 2000.

Oldman, Mark and Samer Hamadeh. *The Internship Bible.* New York: Princeton Review, 2004.

Smithsonian Institution. *Smithsonian Opportunities for Research and Study in History/Art/Science.* Washington, DC: Smithsonian Institution Press, 1972.

Srinivasan, Kalpana. *The Yale Daily News Guide to Internships.* New York: Kaplan, 1999.

International Internships

Gliozzo, Charles A., Vernicka K. Tyson, eds. *Directory of International Internships: A World of Opportunities.* East Lansing, MI: Michigan State University, 1987.

Hitchcock, Laura. *The Imaginative Soul's Guide to Foreign Internships: A Roadmap to Envision, Create, and Arrange Your Own Experience.* Kansas City, KS: Ivy House, 1993.

International Career Employment Weekly (periodical)

Schlachter, Gail Ann and R. David Weber *Financial Aid for Study and Training Abroad.* El Dorado Hills, CA: Reference Service Press, 1992.

Seymore, Bruce II, and Matthew Higham, eds. *The Access Guide to International Affairs Internships: Washington, D.C.* Ocean, NJ: Access, 1996.

Field-Based Internships

Arts, Entertainment, Media, and Sports

Artsearch (biweekly periodical by Theatre Communications Group)

Aviso (monthly periodical; American Association of Museums)

Broadcast Journalism Internship Directory. Arlington, VA: Leadership Institute, 1998.

Entertainment Employment Journal (biweekly periodical)

Gardner, Garth. *Gardner's Guide to Internships in New Media: Computer Graphics, Animation, and Multimedia.* Washington, DC: Garth Gardner, 2002.)

Internships with America's Advertising Agencies. Glassboro, NJ: Career Education Institutes, 2001.

The Media Internship Guide. Glassboro, NJ: Career Education Institutes, 2001.

The Music and Entertainment Industry Internship Guide: For Undergraduate and Graduate Students. Livingston, NJ: Entertainment Media Consultants, 2002.

National Directory of Arts Internships. Los Angeles: National Network for Artist Placement, 2003.

The Sports Internship Book. Glassboro, NJ: Career Education Institutes, 2001.

The Environment

Environmental Career Opportunities (biweekly periodical)

Helping Out in the Outdoors: A Directory of Volunteer Work and Internships on America's Public Lands. Guilford, CT: American Hiking Association, 2001.

Government, Policy, and Social Studies

Frantzich, Stephen E. *Studying in Washington: A Guide to Academic Internships in the Nation's Capital.* Washington, DC: APSA, 2001.

Guide to America's Federal Jobs by JIST. Minneapolis, MN: Sagebrush Education Resources, 2001.

Human Rights Internship Book. Glassboro, NJ: Career Education Institutes, 2002.

Levinger, Carl and Itzchack Schefres. *Everything You Need to Get a Psychology Internship.* Los Angeles: Windmill Lane Press, 1995.

Morgan, Dana and Robert Goldenkoff. *Federal Jobs: The Ultimate Guide.* Princeton, NJ: Arco, 2002.

Opportunities in Public Affairs (biweekly periodical)

Reeher, Grant, and Mack Mariani. *The Insider's Guide to Political Internships: What to Do Once You're in the Door: For Political Interns at the National, State, and Local Level.* Philadelphia, PA: Westview Press, 2002.

Washington, D.C. Internships in Law and Policy. Glassboro, NJ: Career Education Institutes, 2002.

Volunteering

Giese, Filomena, ed. *Alternatives to the Peace Corps: A Directory of Third World and U.S. Volunteer Opportunities.* Oakland, CA: Food First, 1999.

Invest Yourself: The Catalogue of Volunteer Opportunities. Portland, OR: Commission on Voluntary Service and Action, 1991.

Kipps, Harriet Clyde, ed. *Volunteer America: A Comprehensive National Guide to Opportunities for Service, Training, and Work Experience.* New York: Ferguson, 1997.

Pybus, Victoria. *International Directory of Voluntary Work.* Oxford, England: Vacation Work Publications, 2002.

Index

Internet. *See* Web sites for
Internship Bible, The (Oldman), 64
Internship centers for networking, 49, 62–64
Internships, 1–10
   benefits from, 2, 6–8, 10, 71–74
   careers, finding with, 2–3, 4, 6, 7–8
   defined, 2
   famous former interns, **9**
   full-time jobs from, 2, 7–8, 53, 142
   resources for, 157–60
   standing out as high achiever from, 7, 24–25
   unemployment numbers, 1
   See also Application process; Career path, right vs. wrong; Choosing right internship; Dreams and talents, discovering; Employers and internships; Graduates and career changers; Interviews; Networking; Researching possible internships; Successful internships
Internships 2005 (Oldman), 64
"Intern Work Plan," 135, **136**
Interviews, 120–29
   appearance for, 123–24, **128**
   application process and, 98, 99
   asking questions, 126–27
   contribution (your) to the organization, 121–22
   dressing for, 123–24, **128**
   Five Biggest Interview Mistakes, **128**
   goals of internship and, 121
   logistics of interview, 122
   mistakes in, **128**
   mock interview, 122
   multiple interviews, 124–25
   night before preparation, 123
   phone interviews, 128–29
   preparation for, 121–23
   professionalism for, 124, **128**
   questions, answering, 125–26, **126, 128**
   recording information, 129–30
   researching organizations, 47, 68, 89–90, 121, **128**
   strengths (your), 121–22
   Ten Top Interview Questions, **126**
   thanking interviewers/supporters, 130
   tips from employers, 85, 88, 92
   See also Application process

Japan Exchange and Teaching Program, The (JET), 36, 57, 81–82
Jerome Levy Economics Institute Forecasting Fellowship, 80
Job description, passion about, 56–57
Journal, keeping, 144–45, 148, 155

KCP International Language Institute (Japan), **44**
Keirsey, David, 13, 16
KPMG, 94, 97
Kummerow, Jean, 13, 16

La Escuela de Idiomas D'Amore (Costa Rica), 45
Lambert, Stephen, 18
Landes, Michael, 66
Language programs, 43–45, **44**
Languages Abroad (Hungary), **44**
Lee, Spike, **9**
Letters of recommendation
   application process, 98, 120
   supervisors for, 151
Library for fact-finding, 17, 47–48
Liden & Denz (Russia), **44**
LifeTypes (Hirsh and Kummerow), 13, 16
Lobby Corps, 3
Location considerations, 55, 61, 66–67
Logistics of interview, 122
Lorenzo de' Medici Institute of Florence (Italy), **44**
Los Angeles Passport Agency, 31
Los Angeles Times, 67

Macalester College, 29
Major Options: The Student's Guide to Linking Majors and Career Opportunities during and after College (Basta), 18
MBTI (Myers-Briggs Type Indicator), 12, 13–14, 15
Memberships in résumé, 109
Mentors, 139
Microsoft, 2
Middlebury College, 28
Minority Management Development Program, The, 78
Mistakes in interviews, **128**
Mock interview, 122
Money, 47
Mount Holyoke, 29
Multiple internships, 154
Multiple interviews, 124–25
Museum Education Graduate Fellowship, 79
Museum of Modern Art in New York City, 99
Myers-Briggs Type Indicator (MBTI), 12, 13–14, 15

National Association of Colleges and Employers, 8
National Commission for the High School Senior Year, 39

About the Author

According to a profile in UCLA's *Daily Bruin*, Dario Bravo is ". . . probably one of the most important people you'll ever meet."

He has opened doors for thousands of students and graduates seeking high-benefit work experience in the U.S. and abroad. Known by friends as an accomplished chef, Mr. Bravo lives with his family in Los Angeles and continues to advise students daily.

Please feel free to contact the author at La Mancha11@aol.com